THE GRIT, GRIND & BLEED of BUSINESS

Riccardo Marini

Create, Build & Grow

What Entrepreneurs Need to Know…

A Business Boot Camp Guide to Success

It's also a practical guide to living life.

LCCN: 2025923532

JENRICH PUBLISHING

WORDS OF WISDOM

TABLE OF CONTENTS

ENTREPRENEUR'S BUSINESS BOOT CAMP GUIDE

Whether you are a start-up, purchasing an existing business, or a business trying to achieve greater growth, The Entrepreneur's Business Boot Camp Guide provides all the intricacies of starting, purchasing and operating a successful business or taking a company to a higher level.

Introduction

I often wish I had a guide like this when I launched my first business at just 19 years old. It would have saved me from making costly mistakes, some of which came with a price tag in the millions and lessons that still echo decades later. I endured thousands of sleepless nights, faced relentless uncertainty, family consequences, and navigated years of hardships that could have been avoided with the right preparation.

I went through a real-life business boot camp in the unforgiving streets of New York City. Every day was a battle. Every decision was a lesson. And if there were such a thing as a Purple Heart for entrepreneurship, I'd proudly wear it.

But I didn't quit. I built businesses in logistics, banking, insurance, environmental and occupational safety. I bootstrapped when I had nothing. I scaled when it made sense. And I fought through lawsuits, fines, bad hires, partnerships gone wrong, shifting economies, wars, political landscapes, changes in regulations, and pandemics.

Now, I'm putting all of it in your hands — no fluff, no textbook theory. Just real-world experience. The stuff nobody tells you until it's too late.

This isn't just a guide. It's a boot camp. And if you read it like your business life depends on it — because it might — you'll come out stronger, smarter, and better prepared than 90% of the entrepreneurs out there.

Welcome to the real game. Let's build your empire.

Thank you for picking up this book. I salute your ambition, and I'm honored to walk beside you on your entrepreneurial journey.

If I can be of any assistance, you can reach me at Rmarini@jenrichplublishing.com

— Riccardo Marini

Topics we will cover in this book include the following:

1. **Types of business Entities** structures: S/P, C Corp, Partnership, Sub S, N/P, NFP
2. **Types of Taxation** and Understanding Your Financial Statements: Profit & Loss, Cash Flow, Balance Sheets; Key ratios and KPIs every entrepreneur must track
3. Business locations – where should you be? Home, Mall, Main St, Office
4. **Business Valuations:** vs Book Value
5. **Types of Corporate Buy-Out Agreements**
6. **Business Plans** and Types of Corporate Documents Required
7. **Risk Mitigation** and Crisis Management: Business Continuity Plans, Emergency Action Plans, Cyber Security, Pandemics, Weather Tsunamis, and other Contingencies.
8. **Business Financing Options**
9. **Types of compensation:** W2, 1099, Deferred, Dividend, Rental Incomes, Bitcoin
10. **Types of Insurance**
11. **Exit Strategies**… Know when you get out
12. **Discrimination:** Avoiding expensive litigations and claims from employee discrimination cases for wrongful termination, sexual harassment, benefits & compensation discrimination, and many more.
13. **Intellectual Property Protection:** Trademarks, Copyrights, Patents, Trade Secrets, Formulas and Recipes, Registering IP
14. E-Commerce and Digital Presence: Building a website, SEO, SEM, Online Management.
15. Business Automation and Tracking – CRM
16. Leadership Development and Decision Making \: Leading with Vision and accountability, Delegation, Tough Calls, avoiding founder Burnout
17. Time Management and Productivity: Balancing CEO Duties with Operations
18. Customer Acquisition and Retention: Building Customer Loyalty and Word of Mouth
19. Scaling up vs Staying lean: When is it time to scale up and when to battened down the hatches? Franchising, Licensing, and Organic Growth
20. **Business Ethics** and Corporate culture: Navigating the gray area ethically, core values
21. **Advisory Boards,** Associations, Mentorships, and Coaching: who to ask… creating a Board of Advisors vs a Board of Directors
22. **Government vs Private Contracting**: WMBE and winning Govt Contracts.
23. **Franchise vs Startups:** Pros and cons of buying into a Franchise and Regulatory operational differences
24. Green and Sustainability: Integrating eco-conscious practices
25. **Succession Planning,** Generational Wealth, Estate Planning for family or key employees
26, Regulatory Compliance for licenses, permits, certifications
26. Fines, Penalties & Indictments
27. Team Building – what will your team look like?
28. Types of PPE and whose responsibility is to pay for them?
29. Types of Training and Certifications, and whose responsibility to pay for it
30. Types of Security: Employers, Employees, Proprietary Information, Records, and Data Security
31. Types of Record Keeping and length of record retention required by regulatory agencies.
32. Marketing Plans, Business Branding
33. Type of Business Personality

Dedication

I dedicate this book to my family, who endured the difficult times while I was out working, building our future, working seven days a week, fourteen-hour days. They sacrificed as much as I did.

About the Author

Lead with principle, build with purpose, and serve with wisdom.

Engineering Business Success
Through Safety, Integrity, and Vision

For over five decades, Riccardo Marini has been a cornerstone in the evolution of operational leadership, environmental health, and strategic business development across the United States. With a career spanning logistics, mortgage banking, insurance, and environmental safety, Riccardo brings a level of experience, grit, and wisdom that few in the industry can match. From launching entrepreneurial ventures in his early twenties to leading billion-dollar safety operations in high-rise construction, his trajectory reflects a unique blend of hands-on knowledge and executive insight. At the age of 72, Riccardo continues to serve as a mentor, strategist, and safety expert—focused not just on compliance, but on building resilient, forward-thinking organizations.

Riccardo's professional journey began in logistics, as Chief Operating Officer and co-founder at Action Courier International Inc., he honed his skills in operations, team leadership, and transportation strategy. In his nine years there, he led large-scale, multi-regional teams and managed critical logistics systems that laid the groundwork for his future entrepreneurial ventures. With a keen understanding of people and process, he transitioned into financial services, building and working for PMF Funding Corp into a mortgage banking force, originating and selling over $500 million in loans. These early chapters formed the bedrock of Riccardo's business acumen, highlighting his ability to create, scale, and lead profitable ventures.

As his career progressed, Riccardo deepened his impact in the insurance sector, serving as a leader at Landmark Group Inc. and designing HR policies, executive benefits, and insurance packages for corporate clients. But it was his transition into environmental health and safety (EHS) that would define the second act of his career. Driven by a desire to make work environments safer and more sustainable, he immersed himself in training, earned multiple OSHA and environmental certifications, and became a sought-after EHS leader across the New York metropolitan area. Riccardo didn't just enforce compliance—he transformed safety cultures and elevated operational standards at every turn.

Riccardo's EHS expertise is rooted in the real world. Over the past 17 years, he has directed and inspected complex construction projects ranging from EPA Superfund cleanups to 60-story skyscrapers, Army Corps of Engineers projects, hospital expansions, and schools. His work with Green2Green Environmental, Valor Consulting, and Demar Mechanical reflects a portfolio of excellence that spans over $1 billion in project value. He has partnered with the Army Corps of Engineers, NYC Department of Environmental Protection, OSHA, NYC Department of Buildings, DEC, DOT, SCA, and DDC to ensure not only code adherence but proactive safety innovation. His presence on a job site brings peace of mind—not just through enforcement, but through leadership and education.

Equally at home in the classroom as on the construction site, Riccardo is an IACET-authorized instructor and OSHA 500/501 Outreach Trainer. He has developed comprehensive safety curricula, delivered instructor-led training across multiple disciplines, and overseen the accreditation and compliance of training centers. As Director of Training at Valor Consulting and US Safety Training Center, he helped institutions secure vital regulatory approvals and ensured that safety education met the highest standards. Riccardo understands that real safety begins with knowledge, and his ability to translate complex regulations into practical guidance has made him an invaluable educator and mentor.

Beyond the technical aspects of safety, Riccardo possesses a rare ability to connect with people. He has trained thousands of workers—from entry-level hires to C-suite executives—and has led pre-construction briefings, toolbox talks, and safety stand-downs with clarity and conviction. His natural interpersonal skills and commitment to communication have made him a trusted advisor not only to construction teams but also to insurers, auditors, and government regulators. Whether navigating high-stakes boardroom discussions or conducting on-site hazard assessments, Riccardo remains grounded in empathy, ethics, and effective leadership.

Throughout his career, Riccardo has embodied the values of service and sustainability. His commitment to environmental health isn't limited to compliance; it is part of a broader belief that business success must be balanced with social responsibility. From supervising safety on hazardous waste remediation projects to managing training for scaffold, rigging, hazmat, and confined space work, his contributions ensure that people return home safely and projects exceed expectations. His role as a consultant allows him to bring this commitment to multiple organizations, fostering safety-conscious cultures across industries.

Though he has never sought the spotlight, Riccardo's influence has been profound. His work has touched nearly every corner of the construction safety industry in New York, and his contributions to startup growth, insurance optimization, and EHS program development have positioned him as a trusted advisor to both emerging and established firms. He has served as a Corporate Safety Director for firms with over 2000 employees, crafted safety manuals, launched training academies, and managed high-risk sites with unmatched diligence. These roles reflect not just expertise, but enduring leadership.

At the core of Riccardo's journey is a personal mission: to empower the next generation of leaders and prevent them from enduring the hardships he once faced. His mentorship is grounded in authenticity and earned wisdom. He sees board service not as a résumé booster but as a responsibility—to lend his voice, insight, and courage to companies navigating growth, risk, and change. His deep belief in integrity and mentorship defines his approach to governance.

Today, Riccardo Marini remains open to serving on boards across industries, particularly in logistics, banking, insurance, and environmental health. He is especially drawn to startups and businesses in transition, where his experience and mentorship can create measurable value. Willing to travel and collaborate across borders, Riccardo brings not just a résumé of accomplishments but a character of resilience, loyalty, and clarity of purpose.

Character:
Riccardo's integrity is unwavering; he brings honesty and principle into every project, relationship, and leadership role. He believes in earning trust through transparency and leading by example in both words and actions. His career choices reflect a lifelong dedication to doing what is right—not what is easy.

Knowledge:
With over 50 years of multidisciplinary experience, Riccardo is a living repository of institutional and industry knowledge. He stays current with evolving safety standards, regulatory frameworks, and leadership practices, which allows him to deliver valuable insight across sectors. His certifications and hands-on expertise ensure that his recommendations are always grounded in evidence and execution.

Strategic:
Riccardo sees the full picture—connecting operational details to long-term vision and cultural impact. Whether developing safety protocols, restructuring departments, or launching startups, he takes a methodical and insightful approach to achieving goals. His ability to assess risk, design systems, and align stakeholders positions him as a true strategist.

Communication:
A gifted communicator, Riccardo bridges the gap between technical language and human understanding. His success as a trainer, speaker, author, and mentor stems from his ability to connect, listen, and inspire. He fosters collaboration by building mutual respect, clarity, and confidence at every level of an organization.

Personal Mission Statement

Engineering Business Success

As a lifelong entrepreneur and executive leader, I bring over five decades of hands-on experience in building, operating, and scaling businesses across logistics, insurance, banking, occupational and environmental safety, and skilled trades certification training. At 72, I remain committed to empowering growth-minded organizations through strategic insight, operational excellence, and principled leadership. My mission is to mentor the next generation of business leaders, support sustainable business development, and contribute meaningful governance to the Board of Directors with integrity, wisdom, and a forward-thinking mindset.

Chapter 1:
My Early Days... From Refugee Camp to Brooklyn Streets

Let me begin with the early days of my life. I was born in 1953 in a refugee camp in northern Frosinone, a small town in Italy. My parents had just escaped the oppressive grip of communism in Yugoslavia, determined to find a better life. They trekked for five days through rugged mountains and dense forests, surviving on berries, vegetables, and scraps of whatever they could find. Eventually, they crossed into northern Italy, where they were captured by the Italian Army and placed into a refugee camp.

Le Fraschette (in Alatri, province of Frosinone, just outside the city). This site was used during and after WWII and later hosted refugees and displaced Italians in the 1950s–60s.

Veduta parziale del Campo delle Fraschette

Entry into the United States. After five long years of vetting, we were approved. We arrived in America with nothing but hope, moving in with friends and relatives in Brooklyn. We slept on cots in basements, rotating between homes on 75th Street near 15th Avenue, then 19th Avenue, and later Bay 46th Street.

My parents went to work, and my brother and I went to school. My mother found work sewing shoes and dresses in Manhattan's garment factories, while my father became a construction worker. Their work ethic was relentless—Dad rose at 4:30 AM and didn't return home until 7:30 PM. Mom left around 7:00 AM and came home by 6:30 PM.

By 1964, my father bought his first home: a two-family, semi-attached brick house in Brooklyn. I graduated from Lafayette High School in 1971. But while my parents gave me everything they could, they never guided me toward a future—no talk of college, career planning, or life direction. I was completely on my own, and I found that reality to be lonely and, at times, depressing.

My friends were going off to college or working in family businesses. Even my brother enrolled at LaGuardia College with dreams of becoming an aviator—though he later dropped out and joined our father in construction.

At 18, I was lost. I've been working since age 14, doing odd jobs—maintenance, painting fences, you name it. When I turned 16, I got my first legal job at Manhattan Beach Concession, flipping burgers and selling hot dogs for $1.10 an hour. My first raise brought me to $1.60 on the griddle. It was hard work, but the sunsets on the beach and the camaraderie of my coworkers made it worthwhile.

I also pumped gas at an Amoco station on Coney Island Avenue and Avenue J, earning $1.85 per hour plus tips. Later, I worked for Econo Car Rentals, washing and prepping cars for customers at $2.00 an hour. None of these were career moves. I was adrift—a sailboat with a broken rudder and torn shrouds—without direction or destination. The only bright spot in my life was Annette, my childhood sweetheart. I was in love.

Then I heard about a company called Steed Industries, similar to "STP", the famous oil and fuel additive brand that sponsored the Indy 500. Steed was offering distributorships for $5,000 and provided training. I jumped in, borrowed $5,000 from my uncle and aunt, and soon found myself in Chicago, attending a 4½-day communications boot camp called "JL Communications." The trainer, Joe LaRosa, ran a course unlike anything I had ever experienced.

The class ran 24/7 for four brutal days—no sleep, only short breaks every two hours, with one 90-minute rest period each night for a quick shower and coffee. It was mentally grueling. Many couldn't handle the pressure and dropped out. The instructor reminded me of Gunnery Sergeant Hartman from *Full Metal Jacket*—tough, relentless, and intimidating. But I made it through. Ten of us graduated. That course changed my life. I went in depressed and came out reborn, motivated, confident, and ready to conquer the world with fire in my brain and bones.

Unfortunately, Steed Industries was my first business failure. I lost my $5,000 investment, or I stand corrected. I lost my uncle and aunt's $5,000. It stung. I needed to work fast. I was in debt but didn't have the nerve to tell my uncle.

I answered an ad for a vending machine sales job in Yonkers. In hindsight, I must've been crazy—I couldn't even sell a $2.50 bottle of oil additive. Why did I think I could sell vending machines? I got my answer in 90 days: I couldn't. But this failure introduced me to someone who would change my life again.

His name was Harvey Bryant—a handsome, charismatic Southern boy from Oklahoma. He was a golf pro with a swing that shot 70, just shy of the pro tour level. Harvey had the same hunger, the same fire in his belly that I had since my JL training. We quit our jobs, grabbed coffee, and that morning, Harvey spotted a classified ad for a cab company for sale: $6,500 for two taxis and two hack licenses in Mamaroneck, NY.

Within ten days, we pulled together $5,000 each and bought the company. Our competition? Paramount Taxi—with 35 cabs.

We competed by offering better service. Reliable drivers, clean cars, always on time. Then we traded our broken-down Dodges for the iconic big yellow Checker cabs of Manhattan. The locals loved them, spacious, easy to get in and out of, and full of trunk space. I liked them as well. Great viewing from the front, easy maintenance, you could open the hood, and you could actually see the road underneath. They were the tanks of the cab industry; you couldn't kill them, they ran and ran and ran.

Within two years, we had 13 yellow cabs, two Cadillacs for executives, and two limos. We jumped from 2% to 40% of the market. And though we didn't do a single demographic study or traffic analysis, luck was on our side. The area—Mamaroneck, Scarsdale, Rye, Larchmont, White Plains—was filled with executives from IBM, PepsiCo, Amex, Union Carbide, and Dictaphone. I started driving the wives and kids of CEOs. I was requested by name for my professionalism, not just as another cab driver.

Then came the next turning point.

One snowy day, a client called and asked if we could deliver a package to Delaware by 3:00 PM. We made it happen—despite a blizzard.

That was my light bulb moment.

Why move one person in a cab when I could move 40 packages in the same direction? And so, **Action Courier International** was born—before anyone even knew the name FedEx. We delivered 24/7 with a fleet of vans. I could get a package to Boston in 2½ hours—or San Francisco that same day.

We turned our $5,000 investment into over $1 million in revenue within four years.

But then, everything changed.

First came the oil embargo. Gas shortages. We could only fuel up on odd or even days based on our license plates. Gas prices doubled.

Then came the fax machine. What once cost $50 to courier could now be sent for 25 cents in minutes.

And finally—FedEx.

When FedEx launched its IPO, it slashed delivery rates from $59 to $39. Wall Street predicted it wouldn't survive the year. But in a legendary gamble, FedEx CEO Fred Smith—down to his last $5,000—flew to Vegas and won $27,000 playing blackjack. That money paid a crucial fuel bill and kept the company alive.

As Smith later said: "The $27,000 wasn't decisive, but it was an omen that things would get better."

FedEx survived—and thrived.
Me? I learned a valuable lesson: **From idea to empire takes more than ambition. It takes resilience, luck, and relentless reinvention.**

Chapter 2:
When Trust Fails and Sharks Attack

As if things weren't already hard enough, life dealt me another crushing blow.

One day, completely out of the blue, two loan sharks knocked on my door. They weren't there for coffee. They came to collect on a debt that, apparently, my business partner Harvey had racked up from a string of bad bets. I asked them how much—when they told me, I nearly collapsed.

$45,000.

And they wanted it **now**—or else. I didn't ask what "or else" meant. I had a gut feeling I didn't want to find out.

I immediately called Harvey. He admitted it was true. He owed the full amount. I was beyond furious—furious enough to want to strangle him myself. But rage wasn't going to solve anything. I negotiated a settlement with the sharks: $5,000 upfront and 30 days to come up with the rest.

I told Harvey I'd bail him out—but only on the condition that we sell the company. I couldn't stay in business with a degenerate gambler, not when my life was literally at risk.

Out of desperation, I turned to my father-in-law, Patsy Marullo—a kind-hearted man I loved dearly. He didn't have that kind of money lying around; he'd worked his whole life as a painter at the Waldorf Astoria in New York City. But he did have a house, free and clear.

To my astonishment, he let me take out a mortgage on it.

Because time was critical, I went to a BCD mortgage lender—one of those banks that specialize in fast closings. Within 10 days, I had the money. The interest rate was steep—14%—and the monthly payment was $500. For context, at that time, you could buy a brand-new two-family house for $40,000.

I met the gangsters, paid them off, and avoided disaster.

We sold the company for a modest sum. The buyer, a man named Dan Scrofani, offered me a job to stay on. At first, I was relieved—because I had another game-changing idea that could bring in millions in the courier business. I shared it with Dan, and we struck a deal.

I told him:
"I'll run this division; I'll build it from scratch. You fund it. But I want 50% ownership."

He agreed.

"Let's just use my attorney," he said. "No need for two lawyers."

Like a fool, I said fine. **(Note to self: Never, ever agree to that again.)**

I dove into the project with everything I had. My idea came from my previous experience with shipping packages across the country using the airline's *Next Flight Out* service. I spent so much time at LaGuardia, JFK, and Newark airports, I built solid relationships with the baggage claim department managers.

One day, while waiting on a delayed flight, I saw dozens—sometimes over a hundred—bags piled up, unclaimed and untagged.

I asked, "What are all these?"

"Lost luggage," they said. Bags that got routed to the wrong city. Passengers arrived, but their luggage didn't.

Boom. Lightbulb moment.

I asked if I could offer a baggage delivery service on their behalf. Within weeks, I had contracts with almost every major airline at all three New York airports.

That was the birth of **Airport Baggage Delivery Service, Inc.**

We started in a small retail garage. Before long, we were operating out of a 10,000-square-foot warehouse with full loading docks, trucks, dispatchers, and maintenance teams—the whole works. After a year, everything was running like a well-oiled machine.

Then came another blindside.

A close friend, Ricky Russo, someone I had met during my honeymoon and had given a job to as a night dispatcher, was secretly poisoning my reputation. He had been speaking to Dan, my partner, every night between 8 PM and 8 AM, telling him lies that I was never around, that I was off having affairs, that I wasn't pulling my weight, I was off drinking every day.

Then, one day, Dan called me.

"You're fired," he said.

"Fired? I'm your partner. You can't fire me."

But he did, just like that.

I called my attorney, who advised me to immediately take all the company's books and records so he could file a shareholder lawsuit and determine the company's true value.

We filed a stockholder's suit—but Dan fired back. He filed **criminal charges** against me for **grand larceny**, claiming I stole the books and records.

The case dragged on for over a year. I was unemployed, while my ex-partner was sitting on a $2 million company that I had built.

In court, I lost.

Because Dan's attorney—who had supposedly represented both of us—had created the company with **Dan listed as the sole shareholder**. All the official company forms were blank when I signed them. Dan had filled them in later, with just his name.

I was convicted of grand larceny, given a Certificate of Disability, and lost the lawsuit because I couldn't legally prove I had any ownership stake in the company I created.

That was one of the lowest points of my life.

Lesson #3: Don't Ever Trust Anyone Blindly.

Trust, yes—but always verify. Always protect yourself.

Ten years had passed since I first jumped into the working world at nineteen or twenty. In that time, I'd fathered two kids by twenty-three, weathered a bankruptcy, and carried a criminal record. I needed to change something. So, I headed to Wall Street and somehow found myself in the insurance business.

I didn't know the first thing about insurance. Then again, I hadn't known a thing about cabs or trucking either, and after ten years in that business, I could write the manual. I figured I'd give it the same grit and see where it led.

The first 120 days were rough. I burned through two companies—MONY and then Equitable—because I simply couldn't produce. I remember one day I finally made my first sale, I was so excited, I ran back to my office and told the manager I made my first sale for $176.00 in premium. He asked me what the monthly premium is. I said no annual premium; he broke down laughing hysterically. I asked what's so funny, his reply was "we have a $500 minimum annual premium, return the money and go back to work. I felt like a total idiot.

Finally, I landed at State Mutual, one of the oldest insurance companies in the country. And then something clicked. I started selling, then selling more, then selling so much that I became Rookie Agent of the Year.

By my second year, I swept every award they had: the Quality Achievement Award, the Circle of Honor, and the Inner Circle Award. In my third year, I hit the grand slam of all sales awards— the prestigious, international Million Dollar Round Table Award (MDRT). I kept that streak going every year until 1999.

For context, MDRT wasn't just a plaque on the wall—it meant over $200,000 a year in income, more than 100 policies sold annually, and $500,000.00 in annual premiums written. It was a grind and an accomplishment few ever reached. The MDRT was one of the best conventions I ever attended; they were packed with excitement, knowledge, new acquaintances, and the speakers were the best in the world. Then you had the Court of the Table and the Top of Table MDRT members.

To give an idea of how difficult it was to achieve that status, here are the percentages....

Global Membership Numbers

This means approximately:

Out of approximately 5 million agents globally (a conservative figure only 73,458 individuals earned "Member" status in 2023.
ogletreefinancial.com+6members.int.mdrt.org+6redbirdagents.com+6

- **Court of the Table (COT)**: **8,558** agents reached this higher tier.
  skylightfinancialgroup.com+8members.int.mdrt.org+8blog.moneysmart.sg+8
- **Top of the Table (TOT)**: **3,833** agents earned this elite distinction—the highest level.
  blog.moneysmart.sg+6members.int.mdrt.org+6ogletreefinancial.com+6

Percentage Breakdown

- **12%** of all MDRT members achieved **Court of the Table** status (8,558 / 73,458).
- **5.2%** reached **Top of the Table** (3,833 / 73,458).
  These tiers truly represent the elite of the elite in financial services professionals.

Additionally, MDRT itself confirms that Top of the Table qualifiers represent roughly **the top 4%** of all MDRT members worldwide.

But even while I was winning, I noticed my friends in the stock market were pulling in $500,000 a year. I started wondering if I'd chosen the wrong path.

Like trucking, insurance seemed to follow a strange pattern for me—ten good years, and then trouble. This time, it came when my agency decided to relocate from New York City to Colorado. They wanted me there badly. They even flew my family and me out for ten days. Under my management, the NYC branch had climbed from one of the worst-performing offices in the country to the fifth best. I'd built a team of a dozen agents I'd personally hired and trained. But in the end, I turned them down. My wife's family and I were rooted in Brooklyn, and our kids had no interest in leaving.

Then the home office in Massachusetts made another move—literally. They relocated us from the magnificent Woolworth Building to the 80th floor of the World Trade Center. I didn't like the new crowd, and I didn't like heights. Add in a recession, when few people had spare cash for insurance, and I knew it was time for another reinvention.

So, I walked away from insurance and into mortgage banking—without doing a shred of research. And wouldn't you know it? Just as I got started, the entire banking industry was crumbling under the long shadow of the Savings and Loan Crisis, a mess that had begun years earlier… I just didn't realize it until I was standing right in the middle of it.

Has it turned out that if I had relocated and stayed in the World Trade Center on 911, I may have been a pile of dust like the other 3700 that perished. This time I was lucky. There was one other time I was lucky, during the Vietnam War, I had turned 18, and I was not in college, and the country had a lotto system; those who had the lower numbers were the first to go to war. I had number 6000+, I was never drafted, but my brother's number was in the top 100, and he was 23, so off the boot camp he went, but after a few short months, they released him, not sure if it was medical or mental.

Anyway, back to my mortgage banking world, here are some facts…

- The **Savings and Loan crisis** was primarily a **1986–1995 phenomenon** in the U.S., peaking in the late '80s.
- It began when hundreds of thrift institutions (S&Ls) — which specialized in home mortgages — **failed due to interest rate spikes, deregulation, risky lending, and outright fraud**.
- Congress had deregulated S&Ls in the early 1980s, allowing them to make riskier commercial loans and invest in speculative projects, while deposit insurance limits were raised — creating a "moral hazard" problem.
- By 1995, **1,043 out of 3,234 S&Ls had failed**, costing taxpayers around **$160 billion** (about $340 billion today).
- The **Resolution Trust Corporation (RTC)** was created in 1989 to take over failed S&Ls, sell assets, and reimburse insured depositors.

Why the Late 1990s Still Saw Failures

By the late 1990s, most of the *big* S&L damage was already done, but:

- **Lingering Failures** – Some thrifts limped along into the mid-to-late 1990s before collapsing, especially those with long-term bad loans or unsellable real estate from the '80s boom.
- **Bank Consolidations** – Many surviving S&Ls merged into commercial banks, changing the industry structure and erasing much of the old thrift system.
- **Asian Financial Crisis (1997–1998)** – Exposed U.S. institutions with emerging-market exposure to losses. A few small banks and S&Ls with overseas investments were hit.
- **Long-Term Capital Management (LTCM) near-collapse (1998)** – While LTCM was a hedge fund, its near-collapse shook confidence and put stress on some lenders.

- **Dot-Com Bubble Build-up (late 90s)** – Some institutions began making risky tech-related loans, though the major fallout didn't come until the early 2000s.

Key Late-1990s Examples

While there wasn't a *mass wave* of thrift failures like in the '80s, here are notable cases from the late 1990s:

- **Superior Bank FSB** – Based in Illinois, heavily involved in subprime mortgage lending. Problems emerged in the late 1990s; it officially failed in 2001, but the seeds were planted in the late '90s boom.
- **Pacific Thrift & Loan Co.** – California thrift that collapsed in 1999 due to risky investments and fraud.
- **Franklin Bank** and a few others — remnants of the S&L era that went under after years of carrying bad real estate loans from the 1980s bust.

Economic & Regulatory Outcomes by the End of the '90s

- **Industry Shrinkage** – By 2000, the number of S&Ls in the U.S. had fallen by more than 60% from the pre-crisis peak.
- **Tighter Oversight** – Post-crisis reforms from the 1989 FIRREA law (Financial Institutions Reform, Recovery, and Enforcement Act) were in full effect, making thrifts act more like commercial banks.
- **Risk Shift** – Many of the high-risk lending practices that doomed the S&Ls in the '80s migrated into **mortgage-backed securities** and the **shadow banking system** — setting the stage for the 2008 financial crisis.

💡 In short:

The *true* S&L collapse was 1986–1995, but the late 1990s saw the **last wave of failures** from the old crisis, plus **new trouble spots** from global financial shocks and early subprime lending. By the turn of the millennium, the S&L industry was almost unrecognizable compared to the 1970s — smaller, merged into commercial banking, and more tightly regulated, but with risk quietly moving elsewhere.

Who started the fire…

Vernon Savings & Loan (Dallas, Texas)

- **President/CEO:** *Don Dixon*
- Nicknamed **"Vermin Savings"** by regulators because of the blatant fraud.
- In the early '80s, Dixon transformed Vernon into a speculative real estate lender, pouring money into risky development deals and even personal luxuries.
- The thrift made loans to Dixon's friends, political connections, and to insiders with no collateral.
- By 1987, Vernon had **$1.3 billion in assets** and was failing, with over **96% of its loans delinquent**.
- **Dixon was convicted** of bank fraud, racketeering, and other charges. He served several years in federal prison.

Why Vernon S&L is remembered:

- It became a **poster child** for the greed and corruption of the S&L era.
- The Texas S&L failures were a huge share of the national crisis — *Texas alone accounted for about half of the total cost to taxpayers*.
- Vernon's collapse in 1987 helped accelerate public awareness and congressional action, leading to the **1989 FIRREA reforms**.

★ **Quick note:**
Charles Keating had captured all the news; he had *massive political fallout* and congressional hearings, which would be the **Charles Keating / Lincoln Savings & Loan** case in Arizona.

🏦 S&L Crisis Hall of Shame (1980s–1990s)

Bank / S&L	Location	Key Player(s)	Notorious For	Collapse Year	Cost to Taxpayers	Fate of Key Player
Vernon Savings & Loan	Dallas, Texas	**Don Dixon** (President)	Lending to friends, political allies, and himself; luxury spending; 96% of loans delinquent	1987	~$1.3B	Convicted of bank fraud & racketeering; served ~5 years in federal prison
Lincoln Savings & Loan	Phoenix, Arizona	**Charles Keating** (Chairman)	Fraudulent real estate investments; defrauding 23,000 elderly investors; political scandal with "Keating Five" senators	1989	$3.4B	Convicted of fraud; served ~4.5 years before convictions overturned; later pled guilty to lesser charges
Empire Savings & Loan	Mesquite, Texas	Spencer Blain Jr. (President) & insiders	Real estate flipping fraud, inflated appraisals, bribing officials	1984	~$300M	Multiple convictions; several executives imprisoned
Sunbelt Savings	Dallas, Texas	Multiple execs	Aggressive speculative real estate lending; insider deals	1990	~$2.6B	Execs charged; some imprisoned
Commonwealth Savings	Lincoln, Nebraska	Stanley L. Rudman (President)	Embezzlement, fraud, falsified records	1983	~$65M	Rudman convicted; sentenced to prison
Continental Illinois *(not an S&L but a related banking scandal)*	Chicago, Illinois	David Kennedy & others	Bad energy loans; Penn Square Bank fallout	1984	$4.5B (FDIC bailout)	Several execs resigned; no major prison terms
Columbia Savings & Loan	Beverly Hills, California	Thomas Spiegel (CEO)	Junk bond deals with Michael Milken/Drexel Burnham; luxury perks	1991	~$1.5B	Convicted of tax fraud; served prison time

Common Patterns in the "Hall of Shame"

- **Political Connections** – Many executives donated heavily to political campaigns to ward off oversight.
- **Junk Bonds & Speculation** – Instead of safe home loans, these S&Ls invested in speculative real estate, oil ventures, and high-risk securities.
- **Insider Loans** – Loans to friends, shell companies, or the executives themselves — often with no expectation of repayment.
- **Fraudulent Appraisals** – Inflating property values to justify bigger loans and hide losses.
- **Lavish Spending** – Corporate jets, luxury homes, and even art collections bought with bank funds.

🪓 Total Damage

- More than **1,000 S&Ls failed** between 1986 and 1995.
- Estimated **taxpayer cost: $160 billion** (about $340 billion in today's dollars).
- Texas accounted for **about half of the total losses**.

However, I didn't give up, I decided to stay in the industry, and I did well, till another collapse in 2006, and all the banks were in trouble. I would get loans approved, set the closing, and everyone showed up except the Bank with the money. It was time to reinvent myself. This time, I lasted 16 years.

By 2006, the U.S. housing bubble had reached its peak, and the banking system was loaded with **subprime mortgage debt**, much of it hidden in complex securities. The real collapse didn't hit until 2007–2008, but the fuse was lit in 2006.

What Was Happening in 2006

1 Peak of the Housing Bubble

- U.S. home prices had been rising rapidly since the late 1990s, supercharged by:
  - Low interest rates after the 2001 dot-com crash
  - Loose mortgage lending standards ("no doc" or "liar loans")
  - Wall Street packaging mortgages into **mortgage-backed securities (MBS)** and **collateralized debt obligations (CDOs)**
- By mid-2006, prices stopped climbing — in some markets, they started falling.

---

2 Banks Deep in Subprime

- Large investment banks (Lehman Brothers, Bear Stearns, Merrill Lynch) and major commercial banks (Citigroup, Bank of America, Wells Fargo) were heavily exposed to subprime mortgage loans.
- Smaller mortgage lenders like **New Century Financial**, **Ameriquest**, and **Option One** dominated the market with risky adjustable-rate mortgages (ARMs).
- Many loans had **teaser rates** that reset higher after 2–3 years, meaning borrowers would face massive payment jumps starting in 2007–2008.

3 Warning Signs in 2006

- **February 2006:** Housing starts and new building permits began to decline.
- **Summer 2006:** Home sales and prices fell in many markets for the first time in over a decade.
- **Late 2006:** Mortgage delinquencies and foreclosures — especially in subprime — started climbing sharply.
- **December 2006:** HSBC, one of the world's largest banks, issued an early warning that its U.S. mortgage portfolio was deteriorating.

Why It Didn't Fully Collapse Until 2007–2008

- Banks were still reporting strong profits in 2006 because accounting rules let them book long-term mortgage income upfront.
- Most of the losses were hidden inside mortgage-backed securities sold to investors globally.
- The **real liquidity crisis** didn't hit until early 2007 when mortgage lenders started failing, and by 2008, the biggest investment banks collapsed or were bailed out.

2006 in Hindsight

- Economists now see 2006 as **the turning point** — the housing market peaked in Q2 2006, and from there, the decline began.
- If you chart home prices, 2006 is the **high-water mark** before the crash.
- The failures of 2007–2008 (Bear Stearns, Lehman Brothers, Washington Mutual, IndyMac, etc.) can all be traced back to the loans and securities originated in 2004–2006.

♥ Bottom line:
2006 wasn't a banking collapse year — it was the year the **bubble burst quietly**, and the cracks began to show. The real wave of bank failures came 18–24 months later, but the loans made in the 2004–2006 frenzy were the toxic core that brought down the system.

Here's the **Month-by-Month Timeline from 2006 to the 2008 Lehman Brothers Collapse** — showing how the U.S. housing bubble peak in 2006 quietly morphed into the full-blown banking collapse by late 2008.

ⓘ 2006 – The Peak and First Cracks

- **January–March 2006** – U.S. housing prices and construction hit record highs; speculation rampant. Adjustable-Rate Mortgages (ARMs) dominate subprime lending.
- **April 2006** – The Federal Reserve continues raising interest rates (to 5%) to cool the economy, increasing mortgage costs.
- **June 2006** – National home price index hits an **all-time high**. Home sales start to decline in overheated markets (Florida, Nevada, California, Arizona).
- **August 2006** – Mortgage delinquencies start to rise sharply in subprime loans; foreclosure filings tick up.
- **December 2006** – HSBC warns of rising losses in its U.S. mortgage unit — a **red flag** for global banks.

ⓘ 2007 – The Unraveling Begins

- **February 2007** – **HSBC** announces $10.5B in mortgage losses; **New Century Financial** (major subprime lender) warns of bankruptcy.
- **March 2007** – New Century collapses, triggering panic in mortgage-backed securities markets.
- **June 2007** – Two **Bear Stearns hedge funds** collapse due to subprime MBS losses — a first sign that Wall Street is deeply exposed.
- **August 2007** – **BNP Paribas** freezes three funds tied to U.S. mortgages; global credit markets seize up.
- **September 2007** – **Northern Rock** (UK bank) suffers a bank run — first in the UK in over 150 years — due to U.S. mortgage exposure.
- **December 2007** – Major banks (Citigroup, Merrill Lynch, UBS) announce **tens of billions** in write-downs.

🗓 2008 – From Crisis to Collapse

- **January 2008** – **Bank of America** agrees to buy Countrywide Financial, the largest U.S. mortgage lender, to avoid its bankruptcy.
- **March 2008** – **Bear Stearns** collapses; sold to JPMorgan Chase for $2/share in a Fed-backed rescue.
- **July 2008** – **IndyMac Bank** fails; FDIC takeover costs $12B. Fannie Mae and Freddie Mac shares plummet.
- **September 7, 2008** – U.S. government takes over **Fannie Mae and Freddie Mac** (holding over $5 trillion in mortgages).
- **September 15, 2008** – **Lehman Brothers** files for bankruptcy ($600B in assets, largest in U.S. history).
- **September 16, 2008** – **AIG** rescued with $85B Fed loan after credit default swap exposure threatens collapse.
- **October–December 2008** – U.S. launches **TARP** ($700B bailout fund); global markets in freefall.

🔍 Key Takeaways

- **2006** was the *top of the bubble*. The bad loans that originated then were the toxic core of the crisis.
- **2007** was the *year the plumbing froze* — the credit markets seized as investors realized the risks.
- **2008** was the *full collapse*, with failures of Bear Stearns, Lehman, and massive bailouts.

Here's the visual timeline showing how housing prices peaked in 2006, foreclosure rates climbed, and the major banking crisis events unfolded through 2008. It makes it clear how the slow downturn turned into a full collapse

2006–2008 Banking Crisis: Housing Prices, Foreclosures, and Major Events

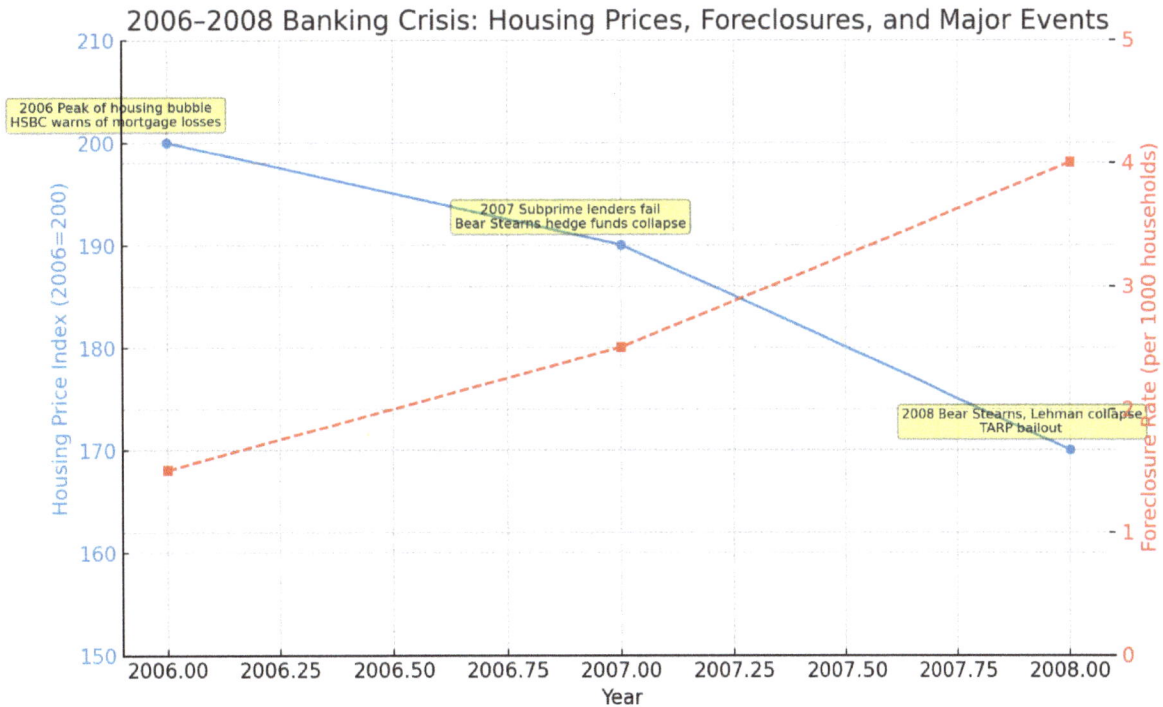

In 2007, I had no choice but to reinvent myself one more time, and this time, once again, without much thought, I entered the Occupational Safety & Health Management Business. Not knowing a single thing about the industry. But fascinating things happened, and I'll get back to this in the final chapter. For now, here are companies that almost went bankrupt but were able to make it from **Idea to Empire.**

Companies That Nearly Failed but Reached Greatness

Company	Near-Failure Situation	Turnaround Outcome
Apple (late 1990s)	Apple was 90 days from bankruptcy in 1997. It had a declining market share and was losing millions.	Steve Jobs returned, introduced the iMac, iPod, and iPhone, and now one of the world's most valuable companies.
FedEx (1973)	As noted, Fred Smith gambled the last $5,000 in Vegas to keep the business running.	Raised more capital; today, a global logistics powerhouse.
Airbnb	Couldn't pay rent in early days; resorted to selling novelty cereal boxes ("Obama O's" and "Cap'n McCain's") for cash.	Grew through persistence and lean startup tactics; now a multi-billion-dollar travel platform.
Netflix	In 2000, Netflix offered to sell to Blockbuster for $50M and was rejected. It was losing money on DVDs.	Pivoted to streaming; Blockbuster went bankrupt; Netflix dominates entertainment.

Company	Near-Failure Situation	Turnaround Outcome
Tesla (2008)	Was weeks from bankruptcy during the financial crisis. Elon Musk put his last personal funds into the company.	Received a government loan and investment; now a global EV and energy leader.
Starbucks	Nearly collapsed during the 2008 recession; overexpanded and diluted brand value.	Howard Schultz returned as CEO, refocused on customer experience; the brand rebounded globally.
Marvel (1996)	Filed for bankruptcy due to poor comic sales and overextension.	Focused on film licensing; launched Marvel Studios; now part of Disney and worth billions.
IBM (early 1990s)	Suffered massive losses; analysts declared it doomed.	Shifted to services and software under new leadership; a case study in corporate reinvention.
Nintendo (multiple times)	Nearly failed in the early 1900s and again in the 1960s after unsuccessful ventures (e.g., love hotels, instant rice).	Pivoted to video games; created the NES and Game Boy; now a gaming titan.
Disney (1930s)	After "Steamboat Willie," Walt Disney faced bankruptcy before "Snow White" succeeded.	"Snow White" became the first animated feature hit, now a global entertainment empire.

Common Themes Among These Comebacks:

- Visionary leadership
- Willingness to pivot or innovate
- Creative financing or personal risk
- Relentless focus on product or customer experience
- Luck

The Story of Black Wall Street

"Black Wall Street" refers most famously to the prosperous African American business district in the Greenwood neighborhood of Tulsa, Oklahoma, during the early 20th century.

Origins and Growth

- Greenwood emerged in the early 1900s as a thriving Black community, built by African Americans who were barred from white-owned establishments due to segregation laws.
- The name "Black Wall Street" was popularized to describe the district's economic success — it had banks, hotels, theaters, newspapers, restaurants, clothing stores, and law offices.
- At its peak, Greenwood had over **600 Black-owned businesses** and was considered one of the wealthiest Black communities in the United States.
- The prosperity was fueled by a self-sustaining economy: money circulated within the community multiple times before leaving it.

The 1921 Tulsa Race Massacre

Here are several historical photographs documenting the aftermath of the 1921 Tulsa Race Massacre:

- The devastated Greenwood District ("Black Wall Street") in ruins, with burned-out buildings and lingering smoke.
- Scenes showing people surveying the devastation, rubble, and the skeletal remains of destroyed structures.
- Haunting imagery of bed frames and personal belongings rising from ashes, revealing the destructive scale of the attack.
- Evidence of mass graves and burial sites underscores the fatal consequences of the violence.

On **May 31 – June 1, 1921**, a white mob attacked Greenwood after an accusation that a young Black man, Dick Rowland, had assaulted a white woman (Sarah Page) in an elevator — an allegation later widely believed to be false or exaggerated.

- Violence erupted, fueled by racial tensions, misinformation, and white resentment of Black economic success.
- The attack involved arson, looting, and even reports of aerial bombardment from private planes.
- Over **1,200 homes and businesses** were destroyed, leaving thousands homeless.
- Death toll estimates range from **dozens to several hundred**, but the exact number remains unknown due to poor record-keeping and official cover-ups.

Aftermath

- Insurance companies refused to compensate victims, citing riot clauses.
- Many residents never returned to their former prosperity, though some rebuilt Greenwood in the years following.
- For decades, the massacre was largely omitted from history books and public discourse.
- In recent decades, renewed interest has led to documentaries, books, memorial projects, and calls for reparations.

Legacy

- "Black Wall Street" has become a symbol of both Black entrepreneurial achievement and the destructive forces of systemic racism.
- It has inspired modern initiatives to encourage economic empowerment in African American communities across the U.S.

- The term is also sometimes used to describe other historic Black business hubs, such as those in Durham, North Carolina, and Richmond, Virginia.

Here's a list of some of the most notable business and community leaders from Tulsa's Black Wall Street before the 1921 massacre, along with what they were known for:

Key Business Leaders of Greenwood ("Black Wall Street")

O.W. Gurley

- Often called the *founder of Greenwood*.
- A wealthy landowner from Arkansas who, in 1906, purchased 40 acres of land in Tulsa, selling and leasing only to African Americans.
- Owned multiple businesses, including a hotel, rooming houses, and a grocery store.
- Helped establish the core of the Greenwood business district.

J.B. Stradford

- Lawyer, entrepreneur, and owner of the *Stradford Hotel*, one of the largest Black-owned hotels in the United States at the time (54 suites, dining room, and pool hall).
- Advocated for racial self-sufficiency and economic independence.
- Fled Tulsa during the massacre after being falsely accused of inciting a riot.

A.J. Smitherman

- Founder and editor of *The Tulsa Star*, a prominent Black newspaper.
- Used his platform to advocate for civil rights and self-defense against racial violence.
- His strong editorials made him a significant voice in the community.

Dr. A.C. Jackson

- One of the most respected Black surgeons in America, praised even by the Mayo brothers of the Mayo Clinic.

- Known for his medical skill, generosity, and commitment to serving the Black community.
- Was killed during the massacre, an event widely regarded as a tragic loss for medicine.

Simon Berry

- Transportation magnate who operated a private bus service, taxi company, and even a charter plane service — all Black-owned.
- Started by operating a jitney service (shared car rides) and expanded into larger-scale transport.

Loula & John Williams

- Owners of the *Dreamland Theatre*, a major cultural and entertainment venue for Greenwood residents.
- Also operated a confectionery and other businesses, contributing to the district's vibrant nightlife and arts scene.

Mabel Little

- Owner of *Little's Beauty Salon*, one of several thriving Black beauty parlors.
- Rebuilt her business after the massacre and became a long-standing community figure.

Black Wall Street Business Directory (circa 1920)

Hospitality & Lodging

- **Stradford Hotel** – J.B. Stradford (54 luxury rooms, dining, billiards)
- Gurley Hotel – O.W. Gurley
- Red Wing Hotel – Owner unknown
- Williams Confectionery & Rooming House – Loula & John Williams

---

Entertainment & Arts

- **Dreamland Theatre** – Loula & John Williams (movies, vaudeville acts, community events)
- Dixie Theatre – Owner unknown
- Williams Confectionery (also a social hub)
- Dance halls, pool halls, and several private clubs

Newspapers & Media

- **The Tulsa Star** – A.J. Smitherman (news, civil rights advocacy)
- Oklahoma Sun – Black-owned publication
- Greenwood Directory & Guide – Community business listings

Transportation

- **Berry's Taxi and Bus Service** – Simon Berry
- Berry's Charter Planes – Private aircraft for hire
- Multiple jitney (shared car) operators

Medical & Health Services

- **Dr. A.C. Jackson** – Surgeon (nationally recognized)
- Dr. R.T. Bridgewater – Dentist
- Dr. E.P. McCabe – General practitioner
- Dr. W.D. Williams – Physician
- Several midwives and home nurses serve the community

Professional Services

- W.D. Williams Law Office – Attorney
- Gurley Real Estate – O.W. Gurley
- J.B. Stradford Law Office
- Several insurance agencies (including the North Carolina Mutual branch)
- Funeral homes (Jack's Funeral Parlor, Darden Funeral Home)

Retail & Commerce

- Over 30 grocery stores (including Gurley's Grocery, West's Market)
- 2 dry cleaners
- Several barbershops (e.g., Steve's Shine Parlor)
- Tailor shops and clothing stores
- Hardware stores and furniture shops
- Confectioneries and cafes (including Little's Confectionery, Williams Confectionery)

Beauty & Personal Care

- **Little's Beauty Salon** – Mabel Little
- Beauty parlors operated by Sarah Page, Viola Smith, and others
- Barber colleges and barber shops serving exclusively Black clientele

---

Financial Institutions

- Several Black-owned banks and savings & loan associations
- Stradford & Gurley investment ventures
- Real estate brokers specializing in Greenwood property

Religious & Community Organizations

- More than 10 churches (Baptist, Methodist, AME, and others)
- YMCA/YWCA branches for African Americans
- Masonic lodges and fraternal organizations

This district stretched along **Greenwood Avenue** and surrounding streets, with **more than 600 Black-owned businesses** in less than 40 blocks.

It was a **self-contained economic powerhouse**, which is part of why it became a target in 1921.

C(IRCA 1920)

PINE

GGOODENNIOOGG (GREENWOOD)		GBEENNNIOION (GREENWOOD)	BOREON	BOETON (BOSTON)	
WEET'S MARKET	DR. R.T.C. MEOBIBNRAR	DL'.F.C.P. McCABE			
STEVE'S SHJNE PIRIOR	GURLEY REAL ESTATE		GURLEY MOTEL		
	STRACFORD HOTEL	(A) LLONHOMA COFFECTONERY	WILLIAMS CONFECTIONERY & ROOMING HOUSE		
	BERRY'S TAALTRUS SERVICE	GURLEY REAL ESTA		GURELY HOTEL	
GROCERY	BERRYS CHARTER PLANES	STRADFORD HOTEL	JACK'S EUNERAL PARLOR		
		GREENLAND THEATRE		WILLIAMS CONFECTIONERY	
WEST MARKET	LITTLE'S CONFECTION		LITTLE'S BEAUTY SALON	JACK'S FUNERAL PARLOR	
STIEV'S SHAMES SRIOR	BERRY'S THARTECA	L/RK'S RAIKD SHOPS			
	D/RAL THOMASES	THE OKLAHOMA SUN	DERRY'S CONTINUD	HARDWARE STORES	
GROCERY	GROCERY	GURLEY HOTEL	SARAH RAGES BEAUTE KARLOR		
	GAISSTRVSTORE	WILLIAMS CONLIOTIONNARY & ROOMING HOUSE	V/OLA SMITH BEAUTY PARLOR		
GROCERY	CHANDRES HARDWARE				
	FURNITURE STORE	JACK'S FUNFRAL PARLOR		CHURCHES	
GROCERY	HARDWARE STORE		CHURCHES		
	GROCERY STORE	DRY CLEANERS			

FIRST

Chapter 3: Taxation

Now that you have selected your entity structure, in the next chapters, we will discuss and outline all the various taxes you will be subjected to, which will affect your bottom line.

Types of Insurances, type of business capital you will need, types of benefits to consider without discrimination against your employees. Yes, that's correct, if you spend $1.00 on yourself for a benefit, you also must spend $1.00 for each of your employees.

We will discuss this further during the employee benefits chapter. The benefits you may consider are retirement income, deferred compensation, health insurance, dental, optical, disability, death benefits, PTO (paid time off), holiday pay, vacation pay, etc.

Corporate executive and employee benefits can be expensive, but a great way to filter cash to everyone on a nontaxable or deferred basis, while receiving a cooperate deduction. Obviously, all of this is predicted by business success and profitability.

If you haven't thought about taxation yet, it's time you start…since every dollar you earn, you will have to share (give away) to the government, leaving you less to work with.

Which brings up another important rule… what state or country do I establish my business in? Not all states and countries tax the same. NYS/NYC is one of the highest-taxed states in the country, whereas some other states, like Delaware and Florida, have reduced taxes, and some have no state tax at all.

In establishing your business prices, rates, and fees, you should pay careful attention to how much tax you will be paying, perhaps implementing ways to legally defer or avoid taxes.

We will discuss legal ways to defer or avoid taxes in a later chapter under corporate planning and benefits. For now, know that you will be paying taxes on income earned, benefits paid to employees like social security, and on products or services you sell. Sales tax, on purchases you make for materials, equipment, supplies, on windfall profits, on savings, on spending, on giving away gifts, on interest earned, on minimum tax regardless of any earnings; the list is long… take careful consideration of pricing your product correctly, considering the total cost of doing business plus your taxes.

Federal Income Tax 2025 brackets in NYS:

☐ 10%: $0–$11,925

☐ 12%: $11,925–$48,475

☐ 22%: $48,475–$103,350

☐ 24%: $103,350–$197,300

☐ 32%: $197,300–$250,525

☐ 35%: $250,525–$626,350

☐ 37%: over $626,350

New York State Income Tax

Progressive tax with nine brackets (2024 income, filed in 2025):

- 4% at the lowest incomes
- Rising through 4.5%, 5.25%, 5.5%, 6.0%, 6.85%
- 9.65% above $1,077,550
- 10.3% between $5 M–$25 M
- 10.9% on income over $25 M

New York City Income Tax

Four tax brackets for NYC residents:

- 3.078% on income up to $12,000
- 3.762% for $12,001–$25,000
- 3.819% for $25,001–$50,000
- 3.876% for income over $50,000

Social Security (FICA + Medicare)

- **Social Security (OASDI)**: 6.2% of wages up to a capped amount (e.g., $160,200 cap has recently been implemented).
- **Medicare**: 1.45% on all earnings (no cap).
- Employers match both (total 12.4% + 2.9%).
- Self-employed individuals pay the full 15.3%

Quick Summary Table

Tax Type	Rate(s)
Federal Income Tax	10%–37% depending on bracket
	The Washington Post+15Wikipedia+15Blog+15
NY State Income Tax	4%–10.9% (nine brackets)
NYC Income Tax	3.078%–3.876% (four brackets)
Social Security (OASDI)	6.2% on wages up to the yearly wage base
Medicare	1.45% of all earnings

Real estate Tax – based on the township's property estimates

Mortgage Tax – 2& in NYC every time to buy property

Water and sewage tax – based on frontage square feet

Notes

- **NY State** has supplemental/additional taxes for very high earners.
- **NYC tax** applies only to residents (NYC + Yonkers add their local taxes).
- **Social Security wage cap** adjusts annually; employer matches apply.
- **FICA**: self-employed individuals pay both the employer and employee portions (15.3%).

Metropolitan Commuter Transportation District (MCTD) surcharge

purchases are taxed at a combined **8.875%** (4% NYS + 4.5% NYC + 0.375% MCTD)

Interest & Dividend Tax

- **Federal**:
  - **Ordinary (non-qualified)** dividends & interest are taxed at your marginal income-tax rate (10%–37%).
  - **Qualified dividends** get long-term capital gains rates: 0%, 15%, or 20%, depending on income, plus potential **3.8% NIIT** if above thresholds (e.g., $200K single, $250K jointly)

New York State:
Interest and dividends are taxed as ordinary income at NY's nine-state brackets (4%–10.9%)

Corporate Tax

- **Federal**: Flat **21%** on C-corporation taxable income (since Jan 2018).
- **New York State**:
Graduated rates—**6.5% to 7.25%** depending on income leveloms.nysed.gov+10NYS Tax Department+10Tax Foundation+10.
  - General businesses > $5M NY receipts: 7.25%
  - Others: 6.5%
  - Manufacturers or tech companies: lower exemptions may apply

Capital Gains Tax

- **Federal**:
  - **Short-term** (held ≤1 year): taxed at ordinary income rates (10%–37%).

      o **Long-term** (held >1 year): taxed at 0% / 15% / 20% depending on income, plus **3.8% NIIT** above thresholds Wikipedia+4Wikipedia+4Investopedia+4.
- **New York State**:
Capital gains are **not singled out**—they're taxed as ordinary income at the same 4%–10.9% brackets.

Luxury Tax

New York doesn't have a generalized "luxury tax" on wealth or spending. Instead:

- Certain goods (e.g., expensive cars, yachts, jewelry, etc.) may have **excise or specific sales taxes**.
- NYC and NYS impose **excise taxes on fuel, cigarettes, alcohol**, but not a broad luxury goods tax, NYC.gov.
If you want details on a particular luxury item, I can look deeper.

Gift Tax

- **Federal**:
  - Annual exclusion: **$17,000** per recipient (2024–2025).
  - Gifts beyond that count toward your **lifetime exemption** (~$13.61M in 2025) and may be taxed at up to **40%**.
  - The gift tax liability rests with the **donor**, not the recipient Wikipedia.
- **New York State**:
No separate gift tax. However, large gifts may affect **estate tax** calculations upon passing.
-
- ☐ **Federal estate tax** applies above a ~$13.99M unified exemption (2025), taxed up to 40% on amounts over the exemption Flash Archive+5Valur+5Landskind & Ricaforte Law Group, P.C.+5.
-
- ☐ **NY State estate tax exemption** in 2025: ~$7.16M, with progressive rates from 3.06% to 16%; note the "cliff rule" if the estate value exceeds the exemption by more than 5%
- The proposed **New York Oil Windfall Profits Tax** (Bill S7953) would tax crude oil producers/importers: it's set as 50% of the excess average price over the 2015–2019 baseline NYSenate.gov.
- **Not yet law**—currently under legislative consideration, not collected.

Communication Tax

- No direct **communication tax** (e.g., on phones or the internet) at the State level.
- These services may include **utility surcharges or franchise fees** from municipalities, but no specific statewide communications excise tax.

Fuel Tax

- **NYS excise tax** on motor fuel: **$0.08/gallon** for gasoline, **$0.04/gallon** for diesel (plus variable petroleum business fees).
- **NYC** adds a **Metropolitan Fuel Surcharge** embedded in local prices, but no separate state-wide fuel tax.
- The proposed windfall profits bill may impose extra excise if passed.

Franchise Tax

- Refers mainly to **corporate franchise taxes** under Article 9-A:
  - **General business**: 6.5% of the entire net income (ENI)
  - Businesses with >$5M NY receipts: 7.25%
  - **Banking & utilities**: separate rates/forms exist New York State Division of the Budget.

Liquor, Tobacco & Firearms Tax

- **Liquor & Beer**: NYS excise on liquor & high-ABV wine = $1.70/L; on wine ≤24% = $0.30/L; beer = $0.14/gal; cider = $0.0379/gal. NYC adds $0.264/L liquor and $0.12/gal beer excise NYS Tax Department.
- **Tobacco**:
  - **Cigarettes**: NYS adds **$4.35 per pack**, NYC adds an additional **$1.50 per pack** (not individually cited here, but standard).
- **Firearms**:
  - No federal firearms excise is collected by NYS, but **applications and dealer licenses** carry fees.
  - **NYC** imposes sales and registration fees for handguns and rifles (fee-based, not excise-taxed).

There you have it, folks — in the end, you keep very little of what you earn. The level of taxation in this country borders on criminal. Don't misunderstand me; I fully recognize the need to fund essential services — public safety, infrastructure, care for the disabled, and support for those who truly cannot care for themselves.

We live here because we choose to or were born here, and most of us love this country deeply. That's why we stay. But loving America doesn't mean we should be expected to bankroll the entire world. Every year, we send **billions** of our tax dollars overseas to fund foreign governments, wars, and political agendas — often at the expense of our own needs.

It's time to fix America first. Our health care system, our retirement programs, our roads, our crumbling infrastructure, our manufacturing base, our housing crisis — the list goes on.

I didn't intend to go off on a tangent, but the point is clear: there is no justifiable reason for Americans to be taxed at the rates we're paying while receiving inadequate services in return. We must stop the endless cycle of international give-away spending, reduce the tax burden on our citizens, and invest those dollars back into the benefits and services the American people deserve.

"We work, we earn, and we're left with crumbs.
America doesn't need to bankroll the world — it needs to fix itself first. Lower our taxes, stop the endless foreign giveaways, and give the American people the services we deserve."

Chapter 4: Business Financing and Valuations

Financing is one of the most critical components of any business venture. I've used just about every fundraising method you can imagine — some conventional, some creative, and a few born out of desperation. The choices you make here can determine whether your business thrives, merely survives, or crashes and burns.

Broadly, financing falls into four categories:

- **Debt Financing**
- **Equity Financing**
- **Internal Financing**
- **Alternative Sources**

Some businesses are fortunate enough to launch with substantial capital. Most are not. For the majority of entrepreneurs, raising **initial** or **additional** funds is the first major hurdle.

The Number One Rule

Before you choose your entity, finalize your structure, decide on a tax strategy, or seek investors, you must **write your business plan**.

Your business plan is your roadmap — a living document you should revisit weekly. If done right, it not only outlines your vision but also projects where you'll be in one, three, and five years. It gives you a measurable way to check if you're on course or drifting.

Think of it this way: if you had to travel from New York City to Frosinone, Italy, you wouldn't just "wing it." You'd have a departure point, a destination, a route, and a way to track your progress. When Columbus or Hudson set out on their voyages, they had a charted course, navigational tools, and contingency plans.

When I started my first business in 1971, there was no GPS. I used a road map to get around, but in business, I had no plan — and I failed. Ironically, I was in the **logistics** business but had no roadmap for my own company. That mistake cost me dearly.

Your Plan Must Be Professional

Your business plan should be so well thought-out that you may want to hire an expert to write or refine it. (We'll cover this in **Business Documents and Plans**.) Keep it visible — not buried in a drawer — and update it as conditions change.

Once your plan is in place, create your **budget**. This should include every single cost of operations:

- Payroll and payroll taxes
- Employee benefits
- Equipment, materials, and supplies
- Software, hardware, and maintenance
- Rent, utilities, and common charges
- Insurance premiums
- Attorney and accounting fees
- Licenses, permits, and filing fees
- Consulting fees
- Membership dues and subscriptions
- Assembly, packaging, and delivery costs
- Marketing, advertising, and promotions
- Travel, entertainment, and client hospitality
- Continuing education, training, and conferences

This will give you your **magic number** — the bare minimum capital needed to operate.

My Real-World Financing Lessons

I've had to raise money in just about every way possible. Sometimes, that meant walking into a bank in a suit with a business plan and projections. Other times, it meant making calls at midnight, selling assets, or getting creative to keep the lights on.

- **Debt Financing**: Early on, I relied on bank loans. One of my first big financing deals was for my taxi company. I walked into the bank with nothing but a belief in my idea and came out with a loan that put my first car on the road.
- **Equity Financing**: I've also given up ownership stakes to bring in investors. That's a double-edged sword — you get the money, but you also give up control. In one case, I brought in a partner who ended up costing me millions and, eventually, the entire business. Lesson learned: choose equity partners carefully.
- **Internal Financing**: When I started my courier business, I used profits from my taxi company to fund operations. It was a calculated risk — if one failed, both could go under.
- **Alternative Sources**: I've pawned jewelry, sold personal property, tapped into retirement accounts, and in one case, secured a short-term bridge loan from a client who believed in me. Sometimes, survival means thinking outside the box.

Bridging the Gap

You may already have the capital you need. You may have some of it. Or you may be starting from zero. Either way, understanding the tools at your disposal — and the cost of using them — is critical.

In the next section, I'll break down **each funding method** in detail — the pros, the cons, and the traps to avoid — so you can raise capital without mortgaging your future.

Your own funds are best

1. **Partnerships or stockholders willing to invest**

2. **Private Investors, Venture Capitalists, Angel Investors**

3. **Crowdfunding Platforms**

4. **Real Estate Financing,** you may own real estate or know someone who does, who has equity in the property; it could be your home, investment property, or your business building; all these properties offer inexpensive financial borrowing terms, like a refinance, or a line of equity (HELOC), Home Equity Line of Credit. Reverse Mortgage, A life estate, a 2nd mortgage.

5. You also need to know that there are different types of lenders and there are different types of borrowers. For example,

   You have A Bank Lenders and you have BCD Lenders, the A lender is your Citibank, or local saving and loan smaller bank which offers the best terms to the best borrowers who have 725 Fico scores and Income and cash, The you have the BCD lenders that have not so great terms for borrowers with lower fico scores like 625, limited income not a lot of cash. The important thing to know here is always match A Borrowers with A lenders and always match BCD borrowers with BCS lenders. Failing to follow this principle will get you denied or stuck with a rate you didn't deserve.

6. **A signed contract** from a client is like having cash. Just take it to the bank.

7. **A billed receivable** is like cash, just take it to the bank.

8. **A weekly payroll** is like cash, just take it to the bank.

9. **Bank statements** showing cash flow deposits are like cash just take it to the bank.

10. **A Line of credit**

11. **A Bank Credit Letter**

12. Inventory Financing

13. Equipment Financing (renting is cheaper than buying, like a car lease)

14. Loans against Savings accounts, CDs, 401 K plans, and other retirement funds,

Loan Sharks — *A Last Resort (and I Don't Recommend It)*

I don't suggest using loan sharks — ever — but I'd be lying if I said I hadn't done it once myself. In that particular situation, the terms my bank was offering were worse. The bank wanted **3% per week** on my payroll advance, while the loan shark was "happy" with **2%**.

You might say, *"That's illegal!"* In this case, it wasn't. The note was structured at 3% per week with a maximum of 12 weeks, keeping it under New York State's usury limit of 36% annually. The reality was, I had two choices:

1. Default with the bank, lose my business, and still have creditors breathing down my neck.
2. Borrow from the loan shark, risk my business, **and** the possibility of "extra charges" — the kind not listed on any contract.

Neither option was great, but in business, you sometimes choose the lesser of two evils. That time, the shark won — and I kept my doors open.

Many Ways to Raise Capital — But Choose Wisely

The real question about financing isn't just *how* to raise money, but **which option is most advantageous**, considering:

- Total cost
- Speed of funding
- Terms and repayment flexibility

Items 6 through 9 in the list above refer to **specialized lending institutions**. These lenders focus on niche financing that big commercial banks like Chase or Citibank typically won't touch.

Leasing — A Flexible Alternative

Leasing can be a powerful way to conserve cash for other expenses. Today, you can lease almost anything:

- Cars and trucks
- Office or warehouse space

- Computers, servers, and software
- Manufacturing and packaging equipment
- Copy machines and other office tech
- Even **employees**

Leasing employees — through staffing agencies — can reduce costs on benefits, sick days, holidays, vacation time, insurance liabilities, and payroll taxes. It's especially useful for **short-term or seasonal roles**.

One important caution: **always** check IRS guidelines to correctly classify workers as either permanent employees (**W-2**) or independent contractors (**1099**). Misclassification can result in fines, penalties, and back taxes. I'll go deeper into this in a later chapter.

Evaluations and Book Value

Let's look at business evaluations, another important aspect, since whenever you draw up agreements like discussed in the next chapter or every time you seek financing or selling of a partial share or the entire business, or get a divorce, the business evaluation is the number people care about. There are several formulas of accounting practices used to determine the value of your business. These formulas are based on assets, liabilities, and revenues.

The terms **business evaluation** (more accurately called **business valuation**) and **book value** both relate to determining the value of a company, but they differ in **purpose, method, and what they represent**.

1. Business Valuation

Definition:
A comprehensive process used to determine the **market value** of a business based on its earnings, assets, market conditions, and potential future performance.

Used for:

- Buying or selling a business
- Mergers and acquisitions
- Seeking investors or financing
- Divorce or legal settlements
- Estate planning

Methods:

- **Income Approach**: Based on expected future earnings (e.g., Discounted Cash Flow - DCF)
- **Market Approach**: Compares with similar businesses sold in the market
- **Asset-Based Approach**: Adjusts asset values to fair market value

Represents:
The **true economic value** of a business, taking into account intangibles like goodwill, brand, customer relationships, etc.

---

2. Book Value

Definition:
An accounting term representing the **net asset value** of a company on its balance sheet:
Book Value = Total Assets – Total Liabilities

Used for:

- Accounting records
- Financial reporting
- Quick internal estimates of worth
- Baseline valuation

Methods:

- Based on the **historical cost** of assets, minus depreciation
- Does **not** include intangible assets unless recorded (e.g., goodwill from acquisitions)

Represents:
The company's value **according to its books**, not necessarily its market worth

---

☐ Example:

Aspect	Business Valuation	Book Value
Basis	Market, income, or asset-based	Accounting balance sheet
Includes Goodwill?	✅ Yes	✗ Not unless acquired
Reflects Future?	✅ Yes (if using DCF, etc.)	✗ No
Market-Oriented?	✅ Often reflects market dynamics	✗ Static, historical data
Use in Sale?	✅ Used to set asking price	✗ Rarely used directly for pricing

---

🔑 Bottom Line:

- **Business valuation** gives you **what your business is worth in the real world**.
- **Book value** gives you **what your business is worth on paper** according to accounting rules.

Example: ABC Equipment Rentals, Inc.

Step 1: Book Value (Based on Accounting Records)

Assets	Amount
Equipment (net of depreciation)	$500,000
Vehicles	$150,000
Cash	$100,000
Accounts Receivable	$250,000
Total Assets	**$1,000,000**

Liabilities	Amount
Loans Payable	$300,000
Accounts Payable	$100,000
Total Liabilities	**$400,000**

◆ **Book Value = Assets – Liabilities = $1,000,000 – $400,000 = $600,000**

This is the value of the business **on its books** (what accountants see).

Step 2: Business Valuation (Using Market & Earnings)

Let's assume:

- The company earns **$200,000 in net income per year**
- Industry multiples are around **4× annual earnings**
- Company also has a strong local brand and customer base

Using the **Income/Market Approach**:

◆ **Estimated Business Value = $200,000 × 4 = $800,000**
(And possibly more if including intangibles like brand and goodwill.)

If we also consider that the equipment and vehicles could sell at a **higher market value** than on the books, the **Asset-Based Valuation** might push this number closer to **$900,000–$1,000,000**.

Summary Comparison

Metric	Amount	Notes
Book Value	$600,000	Based on historical cost minus liabilities
Business Valuation	$800 K to $1 M	Includes earnings potential, brand value, goodwill

---

Final Insight:

If ABC Equipment Rentals wanted to **sell the company**, it would likely list around **$850,000–$1 million**, even though the **book value is only $600,000**. Investors and buyers pay for future earnings and potential, not just what's on the balance sheet.

Once you have this business valuation, you can seek financing that makes sense to the lender/investor. For example, you may ask for $200,00 for a 10% share in your company, but the evaluation comes in at $100,000.00, your investor most likely will walk away. Since he is not receiving his value and he is overspending.

Another thought is, if you purchase a home and it is appraised at $1,000,000.00, would you pay $2,000,000.00? Absolutely not, furthermore, if you were seeking bank financing, the bank would not exceed 90% of the appraised value, no matter what the seller or you agree on.

Chapter 5:
Succession Planning, Generational Wealth, Estate Planning for family or key employees

Succession planning, generational wealth, and estate planning are **critical for both small and large companies**—not only to ensure **business continuity** but also to preserve **family legacies** and **reward key employees** who contribute to the enterprise. Below is a comprehensive guide on what these terms mean, why they matter, and actionable steps companies (and families) can take:

✳ 1. Why Succession & Estate Planning Matter

Whether you're running a small family business or a large corporation, **failure to plan** for leadership transition or asset distribution can lead to:

- Businesses collapse after the founder's departure or death
- Internal family disputes or legal battles
- Tax liabilities that drain wealth
- Key employees leaving due to uncertainty

📉 A 2021 PwC survey showed **only 34% of family businesses** had a "robust, documented, and communicated" succession plan.

🔄 2. Succession Planning: For Business Continuity

✅ Goals:

- Ensure seamless transition of leadership
- Protect enterprise value
- Reduce legal/tax exposure during transitions

🏢 For Small Businesses:

- Identify if the successor is a family member, key employee, or outside buyer
- Formalize buy-sell agreements
- Train next-in-line leadership
- Document SOPs (Standard Operating Procedures)

- Consider the use of **Key Man Insurance**

🏛 For Large Companies:

- Create a formal **succession policy** reviewed annually
- Develop leadership pipelines (bench strength planning)
- Use executive assessments and 360-degree evaluations
- Address board-level succession (Board of Directors/CEO)

📌 Tools: Succession matrix, talent review dashboards, competency assessments

---

👤👤👤👤 3. Generational Wealth Planning

🏛 Definition:

Generational wealth is the transfer of financial assets, real estate, business interests, or other valuables from one generation to another—ideally with minimal taxation and conflict.

☐ Building Blocks:

- Life insurance (term or permanent)
- Real estate holdings and family offices
- Equity in private companies
- Investment accounts (529, trusts, IRAs)

🛠 Tools:

- **Trusts** (Revocable, Irrevocable, Generation-Skipping)
- **Family Limited Partnerships (FLPs)**
- **Holding Companies** (to control assets without transferring them outright)
- **Gifting strategies** ($18,000 annual gift tax exclusion per recipient in 2024)

✨ Best Practices:

- Teach heirs financial literacy
- Involve next-gen in business operations early
- Document a "Family Constitution" or legacy mission

♟ 4. Estate Planning: Protecting What You've Built

📑 Core Documents:

- Will
- Living Trust
- Durable Power of Attorney
- Healthcare Proxy / Living Will
- Letter of Intent (non-legal but valuable guidance)

💼 For Business Owners:

- Include business valuation and shares in estate planning
- Plan for taxes: Estate tax exemption is $13.61M per individual (2024), but sunsets to ~$7M in 2026 unless Congress extends it
- Consider **Buy-Sell Agreements** funded with life insurance, as discussed in the Business Agreement Chapter
- Use **Irrevocable Life Insurance Trusts (ILITs)** to remove proceeds from the taxable estate

---

💼 5. Rewarding Key Employees in Succession

Method	Description
Phantom Stock	Cash bonus mimicking equity value growth
Stock Options / ESOPs	Give employees actual ownership stakes over time
Stay Bonuses	Bonuses awarded after completing a transition period
Golden Handcuffs	Deferred comp plans with vesting schedules to ensure retention
Mentorship Opportunities	Develop high-potential employees for eventual leadership

🔒 This fosters loyalty and reduces disruption when founders exit.

🌐 6. Example Case Studies

✅ Family-Owned Construction Business

- Founder created a **revocable trust** to transfer ownership gradually to his two sons.
- Implemented **Key Person Insurance** on each heir.
- Formalized SOPs and trained heirs for 5 years before retiring.

✅ Tech Startup with Venture Capital

- CEO implemented **phantom equity** for the CTO and COO.
- Set up a **buy-sell agreement** between shareholders.
- Founder created an **ILIT** to cover estate taxes so heirs wouldn't need to sell company shares.

📑 7. What Every Business Should Do

Step	Small Company	Large Company
Create a Will or Trust	✅ Yes	✅ Yes
Document Business Continuity	✅ Informally	✅ Formally (policies, org chart)
Train Successors	✅ One-on-one mentoring	✅ Executive development program
Reward Key Employees	✅ Bonuses or small equity	✅ ESOPs, stock options, golden handcuffs
Reduce Estate Taxes	✅ Family trust, gifting strategy	✅ Trusts, FLPs, charitable foundations

Chapter 6:
Franchise vs Startups: Pros and cons of buying into a Franchise and Regulatory operational differences

Here's a comprehensive breakdown of **Franchise vs. Startup** business models—including **pros, cons, and key regulatory/operational differences**—to help entrepreneurs make informed decisions.

🔍 1. Overview: Franchise vs. Startup

Feature	Franchise	Startup (Independent Business)
Definition	A license to operate under an established brand	A new business started from scratch
Ownership	You own the location but must follow the franchisor's rules	Full ownership and control
Brand	Established name recognition	Brand must be built from the ground up
Model	Proven system and playbook	Freedom to innovate, but no tested model
Support	Training, marketing, vendor relationships	You create all systems from scratch

---

✅ 2. Pros and Cons

🏢 A. Franchise

✅ Pros:

1. **Established Brand Recognition**
   Customers trust the brand (e.g., McDonald's, Subway).
2. **Proven Business Model**
   Lower risk; templates for marketing, sales, operations.
3. **Training & Support**
   Franchisor provides operations manual, training, and vendor access.
4. **Easier Financing**
   Lenders are more comfortable with franchises due to lower risk.
5. **Marketing Assistance**
   National campaigns benefit local stores.

✘ Cons:

1. **High Initial Fees & Ongoing Royalties**
   Franchise fees ($10K–$1M+) plus 5–10% ongoing royalties.
2. **Limited Control**
   Menu, décor, vendors, and pricing often dictated by the franchisor.
3. **Reputation Risk**
   Your business suffers if other franchisees damage the brand.
4. **Restrictions on Exit**
   Difficult to sell without franchisor approval.
5. **No True Innovation**
   You must follow corporate policy—no experimentation allowed.

🚀 B. Startup

✔ Pros:

1. **Full Creative Control**
   You set your brand, vision, strategy, and operations.
2. **Lower Initial Cost**
   No franchise fee; you spend only on what you need.
3. **Scalability on Your Terms**
   You keep all profits and equity.
4. **Unique Brand Identity**
   No association with corporate mistakes or decisions.
5. **Greater Flexibility**
   Adjust pricing, menus, vendors, etc., at will.

✘ Cons:

1. **Higher Risk of Failure**
   No playbook or support; steep learning curve.
2. **Difficult to Finance**
   Investors/lenders may hesitate without a proven track record.
3. **Brand Building Takes Time**
   Trust, customer base, and brand equity take years to build.
4. **You Wear All Hats**
   Marketing, HR, finance, compliance—it's all on you.
5. **Less Buying Power**
   Vendors charge more without volume-based deals.

🔭 3. Regulatory & Operational Differences

Area	Franchise	Startup
Legal Structure	Must comply with **Franchise Disclosure Document (FDD)** & FTC Franchise Rule	Can be any legal structure (LLC, C-Corp, etc.)
Franchise Agreements	Binding legal contracts dictate operations, branding, territory, and fees	Owner determines all terms and policies
Licensing Requirements	May need state franchise registration (e.g., CA, NY, IL)	Only standard business licenses and local permits required
Compliance Oversight	Franchisor audits performance, branding, and vendor compliance	No outside compliance except local/federal regulators
Operations Manual	Provided by franchisor; strict adherence required	Owner must develop SOPs and operations guides
Training & Hiring	The franchisor often dictates employee roles/training	Full flexibility in hiring and training
Marketing Rules	Must use approved materials; pay into national marketing fund	Owner decides the budget, brand, and strategies

💡 4. Questions to Ask Before Choosing a Franchise

1. What is the **total investment** (including hidden fees)?
2. What's the **franchise failure rate** in the last 5 years?
3. What support is included—**training, marketing, HR, legal**?
4. Are there **territory protections**?
5. How easy is it to **resell or exit** the franchise?
6. Are you **ready to give up control** in exchange for stability?

📌 Conclusion: Which Is Right for You?

Choose a Franchise if...	Choose a Startup if...
You want structure and proven success	You want full creative freedom
You have the capital for franchise fees	You want to bootstrap or grow slowly
You prefer support over experimentation	You want to build a unique brand from scratch.
You're okay following strict rules	You value control over systems, vendors, and innovation
You're seeking lower-risk and quicker breakeven	You're prepared for long-term brand building

Chapter 7:
Advisory Boards, Associations, Mentorships, and Coaching

Here's a detailed guide on the roles and benefits of **Advisory Boards, Associations, Mentorships, and Coaching**, including how to form a **Board of Advisors vs. a Board of Directors**, **who to ask**, and how each one can accelerate entrepreneurial success.

🔍 1. Definitions and Differences

🧠 Advisory Board

- **Non-governing**, informal group offering expertise, guidance, and networking.
- No legal authority, fiduciary duties, or voting rights.
- Flexible—can meet quarterly or as needed.

🏛 Board of Directors

- **Formal governing body** with legal and fiduciary responsibility (required in corporations).
- Approves major decisions: budgets, hiring/firing the CEO, strategic pivots, M&A, etc.
- Must be reported in corporate records.

Feature	Advisory Board	Board of Directors
Legal Role	Informal, advisory only	Formal, fiduciary duty to shareholders
Voting Rights	None	Yes
Liability	None	Yes (protected via D&O insurance)
Who Needs One?	Startups, growth-stage, private firms	Required for C-corps, nonprofits
Commitment Level	Low to moderate	High – formal responsibilities
Compensation	Often unpaid or equity-based	Paid or equity-based with defined duties

✅ 2. Who to Ask & Where to Find Them

👥 Board of Advisors

Recruit professionals with specific knowledge or networks:

- **Industry Experts** – offer domain-specific insight
- **Successful Entrepreneurs** – help avoid common pitfalls
- **Finance/Legal Experts** – assist with risk, growth, or capital
- **Former Executives** – bring operational or scaling experience

Where to Find Them:

- LinkedIn / AngelList / Founders Network
- Alumni networks / Trade associations
- Industry events / conferences / accelerator programs
- SBA SCORE mentors / local economic development centers

🏛 Board of Directors

Choose individuals who:

- Understand governance, compliance, and long-term strategy
- Can represent shareholders or investor interests
- Are willing to engage in risk oversight and performance reviews

Where to Recruit:

- Investors or venture capital partners
- Legal and accounting professionals
- Seasoned executives in your industry
- Family business advisors (for family-run firms)

💡 Tip: For early-stage ventures, it's common to **start with an Advisory Board** and later **formalize a Board of Directors** once funding or legal structure requires it.

💗 3. Value of Mentorships and Coaching

Type	Mentor	Business Coach
Focus	Personal and professional growth	Business performance and execution

Type	Mentor	Business Coach
Relationship	Long-term, informal	Structured, contractual
Cost	Usually free (voluntary)	Paid service
Approach	Advice and experience-sharing	Goal-oriented, accountability-driven

🔍 Where to Find Mentors:

- SCORE (free SBA program)
- Industry associations (e.g., NAWBO, NMSDC, NFIB)
- Chambers of Commerce
- LinkedIn groups, local meetups, alumni networks

☄ Where to Find Business Coaches:

- ICF (International Coaching Federation)
- EOS Implementers (for growth-stage businesses)
- Trusted peer networks / referrals

📦 4. Industry Associations – Why They Matter

Joining associations gives you access to:

- **Networking** with peers, vendors, and policymakers
- **Industry insights** and market trends
- **Training** and certifications
- **Advocacy** and regulatory support
- **Member directories** for partnership or contract opportunities

Examples by Industry:

- **Construction:** Associated Builders and Contractors (ABC), AGC
- **Retail:** National Retail Federation (NRF)
- **Tech:** CompTIA, TechUnited
- **Women/Minority-Owned:** WBENC, NMSDC, NAWBO

---

5. How to Structure a Board of Advisors

Sample Setup:

- 3–5 members, 6–12-month renewable terms
- Quarterly or biannual meetings
- NDA and conflict-of-interest agreements
- Clear **roles** (e.g., finance advisor, marketing advisor)
- Honorarium, equity, or networking perks as incentives

Best Practices:

- Set clear expectations (time, deliverables, feedback)
- Rotate members for fresh perspectives
- Don't overload with too many advisors early on

---

6. Sample Topics for Board Engagement

Area	Role of the Board of Advisors	Role of the Board of Directors
New Product Launch	Offer feedback, market insight	Approve large capital allocations
Strategic Pivot	Assess market risks and opportunities	Approve business model change
Fundraising Strategy	Introduce investors, prep pitch	Approve equity issuance
Leadership Coaching	Personal development, succession planning	Review the CEO's performance
Expansion Plans	Connect to new markets or vendors	Approve M&A, joint ventures

ADVISORY BOARD AND BOARD OF DIRECTORS TOOLKIT

1. Sample Advisory Board Invitation Letter

[Your Company Letterhead]
[Date]

[Recipient Name]
[Title/Company]
[Address]

Dear [Recipient Name],

On behalf of [Company Name], I am pleased to invite you to join our Advisory Board. Your experience in [industry/field] and your leadership will be invaluable as we grow and refine our strategic direction.

This Advisory Board will meet [quarterly/semi-annually], and your role will be to provide insights, challenge our assumptions, and serve as a sounding board for important decisions. We respect your time and intend to keep engagements efficient and productive.

Please let us know if you are interested, and we can arrange a call to discuss expectations, scheduling, and any confidentiality terms.

We look forward to the possibility of working with you.

Sincerely,

[Your Name]
[Your Title]
[Company Name]
[Contact Information]

2. Board of Directors Charter (Template)

This Charter governs the operations of the Board of Directors of [Company Name]. The Board is responsible for overseeing management, approving strategic direction, ensuring accountability, and safeguarding shareholder interests.

Key Responsibilities:
- Approving major policies, financial plans, and strategic goals.
- Selecting and evaluating the CEO.
- Overseeing financial reporting and compliance.
- Ensuring appropriate risk management systems are in place.
- Approving mergers, acquisitions, and divestitures.

Board Composition:
- The Board will consist of [X] members.
- Directors will serve [Y-year] terms.
- Meetings will be held at least [quarterly].

Code of Conduct:
- All Board members will adhere to ethical standards and act in good faith.
- Confidentiality agreements must be signed.

This Charter may be amended with Board approval.

3. Advisory Board Engagement Tracker (Template)

Use the following format to track member contributions and meeting participation.

```
| Member Name | Area of Expertise | Meetings Attended | Action Items Completed | Notes |
|-------------|-------------------|-------------------|------------------------|-------|
|     |      |      |     |     |   |
|     |      |      |     |     |   |
```

4. Advisory Board Membership Agreement (with NDA)

This Advisory Board Membership Agreement ("Agreement") is entered into between [Company Name] and [Advisor Name] on [Date].

1. Purpose:
The Advisor agrees to serve on the Advisory Board and provide non-binding strategic advice and mentorship to [Company Name].

2. Confidentiality:
The Advisor agrees not to disclose confidential information received during their term. A separate Non-Disclosure Agreement (NDA) may be executed.

3. Term:
The Advisor agrees to serve for a period of [6/12] months, with the option for renewal.

4. Compensation:
[Optional: Describe honorarium, equity, or expense reimbursements.]

5. No Fiduciary Responsibility:
The Advisor understands this role does not carry fiduciary duties or legal responsibilities associated with a Board of Directors.

6. Termination:
Either party may terminate this agreement with written notice.

Signed:

_____   _____
[Advisor Name, Date]   [Company Rep, Date]

Chapter 8:
Business Plans and Agreements

In this chapter, we will discuss the importance of Business Plans, Agreements, and Contracts. I mentioned previously the importance of a Business Plan, just as important as the other components we've discussed, like business structure and financing. Your Partnership/Corporate Buy-Sell Agreement is crucial to your survival. It lays out in a contract what happens in case of the following contingencies:

- Break ups

- Spouses' relationships with partners

- Divorces

- Deaths

- Disabilities

- Retirements

- Sale of Shares

Obviously, if you are a sole proprietor, this doesn't pertain to you; however, your exit strategy or contingencies should be considered in a sole proprietorship. What happens if you no longer perform the duties of your business? Due to health, disability, retirement... your multimillion-dollar business can dissolve into a pile of rubble and debt. However, with proper planning, you may perpetuate the income flow.

You can close it out, you can sell it, but without you, there may be no business to sell; the term used is a "Key Employee." What do you do with a key employee is the question? Yes, we have the solution... but let's first address Business Plans and subparts of the partnership and corporate stockholders' agreements.

First, we begin with the Business Plan

This is your living business will, your plan from start to finish... If you were in the space business and you wanted to launch a spacecraft into space, you would need a business plan, no different than any other type of business. Let's talk about a space mission...

You first need the plan so you can follow the steps to get to your destination.

- You need a purpose, a goal, and a destination

- You need people to get there

- You need a service or a product

- You need materials

- You need financing

- You need to have certified and trained people

- You need a delivery system or vehicle

- You need a driver, a copilot, a supervisor

- You need to build the vehicle

- You need to test the vehicle.

A comprehensive business plan typically consists of the following **10 key components**, each serving a specific purpose in demonstrating the viability, structure, and strategy of the business:

1. Executive Summary

- A high-level overview of the business
- Includes: business name, location, mission statement, product or service, purpose of the plan (e.g., funding), and summary of financial projections.

2. Company Description

- Details about the business structure (LLC, Corp, etc.)
- Founding history, ownership, vision, and mission
- Description of the market needs the business fulfills

3. Market Analysis

- Target market demographics and segmentation
- Industry trends, growth projections, and size
- Competitor analysis (strengths, weaknesses, opportunities)

4. Organization and Management

- Organizational structure (org chart)
- Ownership and legal structure
- Bios, resumes, and roles of the management team and key personnel

5. Products or Services

- Description of the products or services offered
- Unique value proposition
- Product lifecycle, R&D, intellectual property

6. Marketing and Sales Strategy

- Branding, pricing, advertising, and promotional strategies
- Sales channels (online, retail, B2B, etc.)
- Customer acquisition and retention strategy

7. Operations Plan

- Day-to-day business operations
- Location, facilities, technology, equipment
- Suppliers, logistics, and fulfillment

8. Financial Plan

- Start-up costs, income statements, balance sheets, and cash flow projections (typically for 3–5 years)
- Break-even analysis
- Funding requirements and use of funds

9. Appendices and Supporting Documents

- Resumes of key staff
- Licenses, permits, contracts, legal documents
- Product photos, charts, research, or marketing materials

---

10. Funding Request (if applicable)

- How much funding is needed
- Purpose of the funding (e.g., equipment, expansion)
- Repayment plans and investor return expectations

Chapter 9:
Partnerships

"I hate the word"… most partners do not think about the ramifications of a partner if he becomes handicapped, disabled, dies, or he's a gambler, drug addict, breaks the law… etc.

If he dies, his spouse is your new partner; in most cases, this becomes a nightmare. How do you prevent it? Simple! You enter into a Partnership Buy-Sell Agreement before you open the door on your first day of business. You lay out the responsibilities, behaviors, actions, and events of your partners that would trigger a buyout in a contract. **This limits your liabilities.**

This is a simple agreement…I like to inject responsibility, behaviors, actions, and events. Remember, your partner is the face of your business, and you are responsible for their actions.

Partner A dies, and his share in the business is sold to the living partner at a pre-determined price/evaluation. Both partners ensure this obligation with an insurance company and pay pennies on the dollar. Let's say the business evaluation is $1 million, and each partner's share is $500,000. Both partners get insured for $500,000.00, and when a partner dies, by beneficiary agreement, the shares are bought out for $500,000.00 from the surviving spouse.

The same would apply if a partner becomes disabled, a disability insurance policy is purchased, and when a partner becomes disabled, his shares are sold for a lifetime monthly disability payment based on the evaluation. These agreements need to be revisited every three years since values change all the time, usually upwards, but sometimes downwards as well. Additionally, remember the taxation ramifications of the agreements; if the cost of the benefit (premium paid) is deductible in the annual returns, then the benefits will be taxable. The reverse is true if the premiums are taxable, then the benefits will remain tax-free.

For General C Corps, it operates the same, with a bit of complication… You have three corporate partners, each owning 33.3% shares in the business. Partner A dies, the Company insures all the partners for $1 million each based on the current evaluation. The beneficiary is the Company, and by agreement, they purchase the diseased spouse's shares for $1 million, and the remaining two partners own 50 % of the company. Disability in this case would work the same; the disabled partner is bought out with a monthly income for life in exchange for his shares.

STRUCTURAL SCHEMATIC

A. Partnership Buy-Sell Agreement (2 Partners)

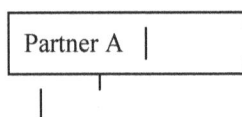

Ownership % | (e.g., 50%)
▼

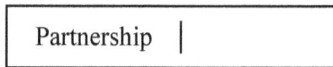

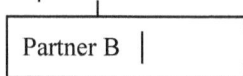

| Partnership | |

▲
Ownership % | (e.g., 50%)

| Partner B | |

Buy-Sell Agreement:
- Trigger Events: death, disability, exit
- Valuation: formula or appraisal
- Right of First Refusal
- Funding: life insurance owned by partners or cross-purchase
- Transfer: Only to the remaining partner or approved buyer

B. C Corporation Buy-Sell Agreement (3 Shareholders)

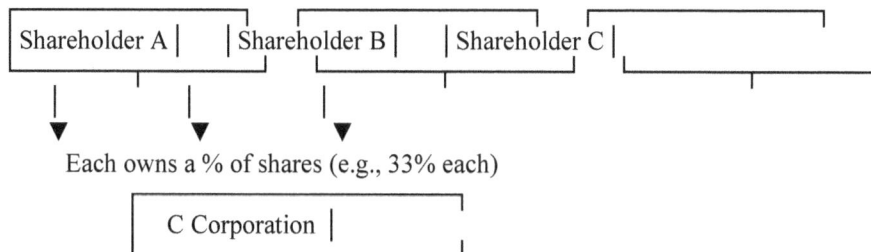

| Shareholder A | | Shareholder B | | Shareholder C |

Each owns a % of shares (e.g., 33% each)

| C Corporation | |

Corporate Buy-Sell Agreement:
- Trigger Events: death, disability, bankruptcy, voluntary sale
- Valuation: formula (e.g., 5× EBITDA or appraisal)
- Transfer Restrictions: Right of First Refusal by corp/shareholders
- **Funding:**
  • Redemption: Company buys back shares
  • Cross-Purchase: Shareholders buy from each other
  • Hybrid: Mix of both (with insurance if needed)

Common Clauses (Both Structures)

- **Triggering Events**: Death, Disability, Retirement, Divorce, Bankruptcy
- **Valuation Method**: Agreed formula, periodic update, or third-party appraisal
- **Purchase Terms**: Lump sum, installments, interest-bearing note
- **Dispute Resolution**: Arbitration or mediation clause
  - Non-Compete/Confidentiality: Optional but advisable

Chapter 10:
Executive, Employee BeNefits & INSURANCE

If you run a successful company and want to withdraw extra discretionary funds without paying taxes while also getting a business deduction, and retain good employees, what options are available?

One of the basic benefits is health insurance. Most companies offer this to their employees in one form or another. It's costly in 2025; a family coverage cost is approximately $1600 per month. That comes with an annual deductible, meaning the first $1,000 you pay out of pocket, then you would have a co-insurance element where the next $10,000 of expenses you pay 20% and the insurance pays 80% Once you reach the %10,000. The insurance company will pay 100% up to $10 million. Some plans have no limit. Then you also may have a doctor's deductible, which is different than your hospital deductible, and also you will have a network doctor or hospital vs an out-of-network, which would cost more.

Since these costs are expensive, you may decide to offset the cost by having your employees pay a certain share, perhaps 25%, 50%, 75% or 100% - whatever you decide. You must treat everyone equally, or that's when a discrimination lawsuit arises. All employees must be treated equally, and as the business owner, you are considered an employee. So, you cannot provide yourself with a 100% benefit plan and your employees with a 50% benefit plan.

Some additional plans include:

- Medical Reimbursement plans

- Dental Plans

- Optical Plans

- Life insurance plans: can come in a fixed amount of $50,000 or 1 x salary, or 10 x salary

- Income Disability plans, short-term, long-term, or lifetime, can include up to 60 % of gross income

Retirement Plans

Another form of benefit offered by many companies comes in various types of plans.

- 401 K
- Simple IRAs
- Profit Sharing Plans
- Defined Benefit Plans
- Defined Contribution Plans
- Key Man Insurance Plans

- Deferred Compensation Plans

All these plans have different results, tax ramifications, premiums, costs, benefits, see comparison chart…

1. 401(k) Plan

Definition:
A **401(k)** is a tax-advantaged **retirement savings plan** sponsored by an employer. Employees contribute a portion of their salary, often with an employer match.

Key Features:

- Funded primarily by **employee contributions** (pre-tax or Roth after-tax)
- **Employer match** is optional (e.g., 50% match up to 6%)
- Investment growth is **tax-deferred**
- Contribution limit (2025): **$23,000** (under 50), **$30,500** (50+ catch-up)

Pros:

- Tax savings
- Automatic payroll deduction
- Employer contributions

Cons:

- Early withdrawal penalties before age 59½
- Subject to required minimum distributions (RMDs)

2. Profit Sharing Plan

Definition:
A **Profit-Sharing Plan** is a type of retirement plan where an employer **contributes a portion of profits** to employee accounts. Contributions are discretionary and not required every year.

Key Features:

- Employer-funded only
- No employee contribution required
- Allocation can be proportional or based on a formula
- Contribution limit (2025): **Up to 25% of compensation or $69,000**, whichever is less

Pros:

- Flexible contributions (good in variable profit years)
- Helps retain employees
- Tax-deductible to the employer

Cons:

- May require annual nondiscrimination testing
- Vesting schedules may apply

---

3. Defined Benefit Plan

Definition:
A **Defined Benefit Plan** (traditional pension) guarantees a **fixed monthly benefit** at retirement, usually based on salary and years of service.

Key Features:

- Employees promise a specific benefit (e.g., $3,000/month)
- Employer funds bear investment risk
- Actuarial valuations required annually
- Can be combined with a 401(k)

Pros:

- Predictable retirement income
- High contribution limits (especially for older business owners)

Cons:

- Expensive and complex to maintain
- Requires consistent annual funding

---

4. Defined Contribution Plan

Definition:
A **Defined Contribution Plan** is a retirement plan where the **employer and/or employee contributes a set amount** into an individual account. The **retirement benefit depends on investment performance**.

Examples: 401(k), SEP IRA, SIMPLE IRA, Profit Sharing

Key Features:

- Employee owns account
- Employer contribution may be fixed or match-based
- No guaranteed payout at retirement
- Contribution limit similar to 401(k): **$69,000 (2025 combined limit)**

Pros:

- More flexible for employers
- Employees control investments

Cons:

- No guaranteed benefit
- Investment risk is on the employee

---

5. Key Man Insurance Plan

Definition:
Key Man (Key Person) Insurance is a life (or disability) insurance policy a business takes out on a **critical employee or owner**. The company is the **owner, beneficiary, and payer** of the policy.

Key Features:

- Protects against financial loss due to the death or disability of a key person
- Death benefit helps fund recruitment, business continuity, or debt repayment
- Often required by lenders/investors

Pros:

- Business continuity protection
- Can be used to fund buy-sell agreements

Cons:

- Premiums are not tax-deductible
- May require medical underwriting

---

6. Deferred Compensation Plan

Definition:
A **Deferred Compensation Plan** is a written agreement between employer and employee to **delay a portion of the employee's income** until a future date (e.g., retirement, separation, or death).

Two types:

- **Qualified** (e.g., 401(k)) – regulated and tax-advantaged
- **Nonqualified** – used for executives; fewer restrictions, not ERISA-protected

Key Features:

- Deferral of income taxes until paid
- Often used to **retain key executives**
- Benefits can be forfeitable (golden handcuffs)

Pros:

- Reduces current taxable income
- Flexible structuring for executives

Cons:

- Unsecured promise—risk if the company fails
- Complicated legal/tax structuring (especially for non-qualified plans)

This activity, perpetuated by employers and employees, has brought down many a company or, at best, cost millions of dollars. What are the various types of discrimination charges against companies?

Discrimination cases brought against companies typically fall under federal, state, or local anti-discrimination laws—most notably Title VII of the Civil Rights Act of 1964, the Americans with Disabilities Act (ADA), the Age Discrimination in Employment Act (ADEA), and others. Here are the **most common types of discrimination cases** brought against employers:

1. Race and Color Discrimination

- Treating an employee or applicant unfavorably because of their race or characteristics associated with race (hair texture, skin tone, facial features).

- Includes racial slurs, offensive or derogatory remarks, or unequal treatment in hiring, promotions, or discipline.

2. Sex and Gender Discrimination

- Includes discrimination based on sex, gender identity, or sexual orientation.
- Covers unequal pay, hiring/firing decisions, promotion denial, sexual harassment, and gender stereotyping.

3. Age Discrimination

- Under the ADEA, it's illegal to discriminate against employees aged 40 or older.
- Common claims: forced early retirement, demotions, denial of training or promotion, or termination based on age.

4. Disability Discrimination

- Under the ADA, employers must provide reasonable accommodations to qualified individuals with disabilities unless it causes undue hardship.
- Claims include failure to accommodate, wrongful termination, or harassment due to a disability.

5. Religious Discrimination

- Treating a person unfavorably due to religious beliefs or practices.
- Employers must accommodate religious practices unless it causes undue hardship (e.g., flexible scheduling, dress code exceptions).

6. National Origin Discrimination

- Discrimination based on a person's country of origin, ethnicity, accent, or cultural traits.
- Includes English-only rules, hostile work environment, or differential treatment.

7. Pregnancy Discrimination

- Protected under the Pregnancy Discrimination Act.
- Involves unfair treatment related to pregnancy, childbirth, or related medical conditions, including refusal to provide modified duties or leave.

8. Sexual Orientation and Gender Identity Discrimination

- Protected under Title VII (per Supreme Court ruling, 2020).
- Includes discrimination against LGBTQ+ employees in any aspect of employment.

9. Genetic Information Discrimination

- Under the Genetic Information Nondiscrimination Act (GINA), it is unlawful to use genetic information (family medical history, DNA tests) to make employment decisions.

10. Retaliation

- Occurs when an employer punishes an employee for asserting their rights to be free from discrimination or harassment.
- Retaliation is the **most common** type of claim filed with the EEOC.

11. Wrongful Termination.

- Occurs when you terminate an employee for the wrong reason. You can justifiably terminate them for no reason or at will, but do not terminate him if he has a criminal record that's not a murder, bank robber, or rape charge.

Less Common but Possible Claims:

- **Marital Status Discrimination**
- **Criminal Record Discrimination** (depending on state law)
- **Military or Veteran Status Discrimination**

Examples of Legal Remedies in These Cases:

- Reinstatement of employment
- Back pay and front pay
- Compensatory and punitive damages
- Attorney's fees and court costs
- Policy changes and mandatory training

I was witness to an insurance company executive who asked a black receptionist to lunch and cocktails, and she played along because she knew she would receive a large bonus when she filed the discrimination lawsuit. He was naïve, she was attractive, smart, and he offered her special treatment if they entered a sexual relationship. She quit her job, filed a lawsuit, and was settled in months for $100K. 100K, He kept his job, she was gone. That being said, she may do this twice a year and make more money, and rightfully so, than a receptionist.

I personally filed two wrongful discrimination lawsuits and won both. The message is very clear: DO NOT DISCRIMINATE against employees.

When is it Legal?

1. **Separate Legal Entities**
   - If companies are set up as **separate legal entities** (e.g., separate LLCs, corporations), they can have different compensation packages, benefits, and policies.
2. **No Discrimination or Violation of Employment Law**
   - Differences in benefits **must not discriminate** against protected classes (e.g., race, gender, age, etc.).
   - Benefits policies must be applied consistently within each company to avoid **internal discrimination claims**.
3. **No Breach of Fiduciary Duties**
   - Corporate officers must act in the best interest of each company individually. Favoring one company **at the expense of another** could breach fiduciary duties if it causes harm to shareholders or stakeholders.
4. **Compliant with ERISA and Tax Law**
   - If offering retirement or health benefits, the plans must comply with **IRS and ERISA rules**. Some rules (like nondiscrimination rules) apply if the companies are considered a **controlled group**.

⚠ Potential Legal and Tax Issues:

1. **Controlled Group Rules (IRS/ERISA)**
   - If the companies are under **common ownership**, they may be considered a **controlled group** for benefit plan purposes.

67

- o This means you may be **required to include employees from both companies** in retirement or health benefit plans to avoid discrimination against rank-and-file employees.

2. **Self-Dealing or Preferential Treatment**
   - o If one company is benefiting the other in a way that isn't at "arm's length," such as through unfair pricing, subsidies, or hidden transfers of value, it could raise **tax issues or shareholder disputes**.

3. **Intercompany Agreements**
   - o If benefits or services are shared (e.g., HR, insurance, facilities), there should be **written intercompany agreements** to formalize the relationship and prevent tax or legal issues.

4. **Labor Law Considerations**
   - o In unionized workplaces, offering different benefits could violate a collective bargaining agreement or be considered **union avoidance tactics**.

Example:

If Company A (a facade restoration business) and Company B (a training school) are both owned by the same individuals:

- It is legal for Company B to offer tuition reimbursement or free training to its employees, while Company A does not.
- But if Company B offers retirement benefits and Company A excludes employees who do similar work, the IRS may require inclusion under...

"Controlled Group Testing"

Summary:

Action	Legal?	Conditions
Different benefits across separate companies	✓	Must not discriminate illegally or violate ERISA/IRS rules
Favoring one company financially	⚠	May raise fiduciary, tax, or shareholder concerns
Sharing benefits between companies	⚠	Requires clear documentation and compliance with benefit regulations

Chapter 11:
Risk Mitigation and Crisis Management

RM and Cm are critical components of any company; they take into account the prevention of losses due to unforeseen events. So what could possibly go wrong, you ask? There have been many companies that had to close their doors because of the unforeseen events I will describe.

Why is crisis management vital?

- **<u>Damaged Reputation</u>:** A crisis can ruin your brand image and company reputation. What does this imply? Customers won't patronize your business at all.
- **Disrupted Operations:** A crisis can disrupt your day-to-day operations. It can delay your products or services, compromise consumer needs, and affect business profitability.
- **Employee Turnover:** A crisis can make your employees lose their trust and confidence in your organization. Chances are, they'll resign from work!
- **Consumer Distrust**: A crisis can drive customers away. Who wants to deal with a company involved in an issue or scandal anyway?
- **Poor Sales Revenue**: A crisis leads to poor productivity and customer dissatisfaction. That can significantly hurt your sales!
- **Financial Losses:** A crisis doesn't only require time and effort to mitigate its risk. It also involves money, whether to manage it or pay a hefty penalty.
- **Legal Implications:** A crisis can make your business subject to legal consequences. It happens when you fail to comply with legal and regulatory requirements.
- **Business Closure:** A crisis can go as far as shutting down your business. It occurs when you can no longer manage the crisis.

Given the negative impact of corporate crises, companies and organizations are investing in crisis management. The proof is in the numbers: *The crisis management market could grow from $110 billion in 2022 to $220 billion by 2032. It's forecasted to expand at a 5% compound annual growth rate (CAGR).*

Every year, hundreds of companies face major scandals and crises that require a significant amount of damage control. There is a lot that PR and marketing professionals can learn from these situations and the selected response.

In addition, we have had:

1. **PANDEMICS (2019 Covid).**

2. **Active Shooters across the nation**,

3. **Civil Unrest Riots rampaging across America, looting, burning, and destroying infrastru**cture everywhere, closing businesses forever.

4. **Storms, Hurricanes, Floods.** SANDY destroyed millions of businesses

Here are some crises and key takeaways that every leader can use to improve their crisis response management process.

The COVID-19 pandemic resulted in net losses starting at $3.2 trillion and reaching as much as $4.8 trillion in U.S. real gross domestic product over the course of two years, a USC study finds.

The pandemic's economic impact depends on factors such as the duration and extent of the business closures, the gradual reopening process, infection rates and fatalities, avoiding public places, and pent-up consumer demand, according to research by the USC Center for Risk and Economic Analysis of Terrorism Events (CREATE).

. BP Deepwater Horizon oil spill

> **Date:** April 2010

Oil and gas giant BP kicked off the decade with one of the worst environmental disasters in history. In April 2010, the BP-licensed oil drilling rig Deepwater Horizon exploded, killing 11 workers. The rig sank into the Gulf of Mexico, breaking the well open and spilling oil. In what is now estimated to be the largest marine oil spill in history, between 2.5 and 4.2 million barrels of oil flowed into the ocean over an 87-day period before the well was capped, forming an oil slick thousands of square miles wide.

The spill had catastrophic economic and environmental impacts, from reduced beach tourism to an estimated fish and wildlife death toll in the hundreds of thousands. Total costs stood at $65 billion as of the end of last year. The incident ultimately led to a temporary moratorium on offshore drilling.

Foxconn suicides
> **Date:** 2010

In 2010, there were 14 confirmed suicides at the flagship plant of Foxconn, a Chinese company that manufactures an estimated 40% of the world's consumer electronics, including components for the iPhone, PlayStation 4, and Xbox One.

The suicides garnered substantial press coverage in the United States and drew attention to the poor labor conditions at the factory. Interviews with Foxconn employees and other investigations revealed that the average worker works in 12-hour-long shifts and receives a cafeteria meal allowance worth just 65 cents, and that many of the suicides were committed in protest of the work conditions.

The scandal threatened to tarnish the reputations of some of Foxconn's U.S. customers, including Apple and Hewlett-Packard, who conducted audits of the factory's labor conditions in March 2010. Since 2010, at least eight additional suicides at the factory have been reported.

CBS sexual harassment scandal
> **Date:** November 2017-September 2018

One of the defining cultural trends of the 2010s was the widespread organization and empowerment of victims of sexual harassment and assault. Under the banner of the #MeToo movement, millions of victims have broken the silence on their stories of abuse, leading to the ouster of some of the most powerful men in politics and industry, and a measurable improvement in sexual harassment awareness.

One of the largest institutions that faced widespread accusations of sexual misconduct was CBS. Major figures — CEO Les Moonves, longtime anchor Charlie Rose, and executive producer Jeff Fager — lost their jobs after being accused of sexual misconduct, and a number of employees have spoken out about the company's hostile culture.

Volkswagen emissions scandal
> **Date:** September 2015

News of one of the largest corporate scandals of the decade broke on Sept. 18, 2015, when the Environmental Protection Agency ordered Volkswagen to recall some 482,000 diesel passenger cars sold in the United States. The notice of violation came after researchers discovered that a number of Volkswagen models were emitting illegally high levels of poisonous nitrogen oxides, and that the polluting vehicles contained illegal software that could detect when the cars were being tested and change the performance to pass the emissions tests. It has since been revealed that 11 million vehicles contain the software.

VW was ordered to pay more than $25 billion in fines in the United States and reported an operating loss of $1.77 billion in 2015. According to a study published in Environmental Research Letters, 59 premature deaths will result from the excess pollution of illegal VW cars in the United States alone.

Turing Pharmaceuticals' HIV drug price gouging
> **Date:** September 2015

Former Turing Pharmaceuticals CEO Martin Shkreli in 2015 increased the cost of the life-saving drug Daraprim by 5,000%, driving the price of the drug from $13.50 to $750 per pill. Daraprim, which costs less than a dollar to manufacture, is a medicine for toxoplasmosis, which can lead to deadly infections in people with HIV and affects about 2,000 Americans per year. The price hike caused widespread outrage. Shkreli was required to testify in front of Congress over the company's pricing tactics and was eventually convicted in an unrelated case of securities fraud for which he is currently serving a seven-year prison sentence.

The Martin Shkreli scandal was big news on its own, but it was by no means an isolated problem throughout the decade. To give just one example, it was just one year later that pharmaceutical company Mylan boosted prices by 400% for its EpiPen auto injector, a life-saving medicine for cases of severe allergic reactions.

Theranos
> **Date:** October 2015

In the approximately 15 years Theranos was in operation, the health technology company was able to raise more than $700 million in venture capital and reach a peak valuation of $10 billion without publishing a single scientific research paper. The company was led by founder Elizabeth Holmes, who started Theranos at age 19 and was a frequent subject of praise by media outlets like The New Yorker, Forbes, and Fortune.

The company touted technology that could perform a wide range of lab tests with a single drop of blood, but an October 2015 expose in The Wall Street Journal claimed Theranos had deceived the public. This opened the company to further scrutiny. The fallout began shortly thereafter, and Holmes was charged with massive fraud in March 2018. The former wunderkind is currently set to stand trial in federal court in 2020 and will face penalties of up to 20 years in prison and tens of millions of dollars in fines.

Fyre Festival
> **Date:** April 2017

Hundreds of festival goers arrived on April 27, 2017, on the Bahamian island of Grand Exuma to attend the much-hyped Fyre Festival. The event, which was promoted by some of the world's biggest supermodels, advertised a music festival with top-tier musical talent, drinks on a white sand beach, gourmet food, and luxury villas. Guests, however, arrived to find that the festival site was an unbuilt housing development; dinner consisted of a slice of bread, two slices of cheese, and salad; and many of the shelters were half-built FEMA disaster relief tents.

The scandal was broadcast to the world in real time. Festival guests tweeted images of a free-for-all grab and dash for shelter, outbound attendees locked in Exuma International Airport with no food, water, or air conditioning, and other footage of the bedlam that quickly unfolded. In the fallout from the festival, organizer Billy McFarland was sentenced to six years in prison on two counts of wire fraud and ordered to pay $26 million in restitution. He is also currently facing several class action lawsuits. While some attendees may have received refunds through their credit card companies, as of the beginning of this year, no one at the festival had been refunded.

Wells Fargo account fraud
> **Date:** September 2016

The Consumer Financial Protection Bureau revealed on Sept. 8, 2016, that Wells Fargo employees had opened more than 2 million unauthorized deposit and credit card accounts. In order to reach sales targets and other incentives, thousands of employees had opened accounts without customer consent. They also transferred funds from authorized accounts into the unauthorized accounts, which racked up fees and other charges for the unsuspecting customers.

Wells Fargo has been hit with over $2 billion in penalties related to the phony accounts since the scandal broke. Over 5,000 employees were fired in connection with the fake accounts, and CEO John Stumpf was forced to retire. Credit card applications plummeted in October 2016, and the Better Business Bureau revoked its accreditation of the bank.

College admissions scandal
> **Date: March 2019**

With such developments over the decade as rising pay for university presidents, which now often exceeds $1 million, labor strikes by workers building university campuses overseas, and declines in government funding of higher education, it seems higher education in the United States has increasingly become big business.

The college admissions scandal of 2019 might be considered a corporate scandal in light of these trends. Unsealed court documents filed by FBI agents investigating corporate fraud implicated 32 individuals, including officials at eight elite universities: Georgetown, the University of Southern California, Stanford, Yale, and Wake Forest University. The scandal also involved 52 people accused of bribing or cheating their children into college. As of October, seven individuals had received jail sentences of weeks or months.

WeWork IPO disaster
> **Date:** August 2019

Office-sharing real estate company WeWork filed in August 2019 its highly anticipated S-1 form with the Securities and Exchange Commission in preparation to become a public company. However, a litany of red flags in the document — including massive losses, expensive lease agreements, complex corporate structure, an all-male board of directors, and CEO Adam Neumann's outsized control of the company — was seen as major risks by investors and invited further scrutiny into the company's leadership. Examples of Neumann's lifestyle and idiosyncrasies that came to light as the IPO collapsed added to the scandal. The disgraced CEO was reported to have illegally transported marijuana in his private jet across international borders and promoted excessive alcohol consumption in professional settings. He banned meat at his company, considered running for president of the world, and expressed a desire to become the world's first trillionaire.

Amid a storm of negative press, WeWork slashed its valuation from $47 billion to $10 billion, ousted its CEO, and laid off 2,400 employees — nearly one-fifth of its workforce. The IPO — which has been delayed indefinitely — ultimately cast a shadow on spendthrift, fast-growth startups and has likely soured the marketplace on future unicorn IPOs.

Johnson & Johnson baby powder recall
> **Date:** October 2019

On Oct. 18, 2019, Johnson & Johnson recalled 33,000 bottles of baby powder after the Food and Drug Administration discovered traces of asbestos in the product. The recall comes after decades of concern — from both the public and from within the company — that the baby powder could contain the cancer-causing mineral.

At the time of the recall, J&J faced more than 15,000 lawsuits from customers who alleged the baby powder caused them to develop cancer. While the company is currently fighting the accusations and has declared the product is completely safe, analysts estimate the lawsuits could cost the company up to $10 billion.

NYC July 2025 - shooting at Blackstone building live updates: Shane Tamura killed four bystanders and hero cop Didarul Islam, NYPD says.

Islam, a 36-year-old four-year veteran of the force, was Shane Tamura's first victim after the crazed gunman stormed 345 Park Avenue Monday evening, where the off-duty Finest was working as a security detail.

The deranged Tamura also fatally shot security guard Aland Etienne, 43-year-old Blackstone executive Wesley LePatner, before taking the elevator to the 33rd floor, where he shot and killed Rudin Management employee Julia Hyman before turning the gun on himself.

The list is endless… What can be done to prevent these catastrophic events? …

With active shooters, creating a hardened border. Let the cameras and software do the work.

IT'S CALLED PLANNING and EXECUTION. Here are some suggestions:

1) Business Contingency Plan

2) Emergency Evacuation Plan

3) Business Continuation Plan

4) Health and Safety Plan

5) Active Shooter Plan

6) Risk Mitigation Plan

The workplace should be a safe space for workers to earn a living, but not all the time do employees feel safe at work. Harassment has always been a major concern faced by even top brands and big organizations.

In fact, over half of employees have encountered **inappropriate, unethical, or illegal behaviors at work,** with the following as the most prevalent:

- Bullying (51%)

- Sexual harassment (40%)

- Racism (30%).

Solutions:
- Investigate harassment allegations in the workplace.

- Identify perpetrators or culprits and issue them proper disciplinary actions.

- Review and update company policies, particularly the employee code of conduct.

- Provide regular orientation and training to prevent future incidents.

- Foster your employees' overall well-being and promote a culture of safety.

Whether a fire outbreak, a sudden earthquake, or a devastating storm, the key here is to establish a contingency plan for potential disruption.

Solutions:
- Act on the disaster immediately by activating your contingency measures.

- Implement your **disaster recovery plans** as soon as the disaster ends.

- Ensure the safety of your employees and other affected stakeholders.

- Work on restoring the disrupted operations as soon as possible.

- Review and improve your contingency plans for potential disasters in the future.
- **Perform emergency exercises** to acclimate the workers to possible real-life craziness and how to manage it. This is an important part since it can result in a smooth transition and save lives and prevent injuries.

A corporate crisis is inevitable, as it can strike anytime and anywhere. Whether it's a product recall, an employee strike, a natural calamity, an employee gone mad, an executive misconduct, riots, or whatever, you must come in prepared and ready.

That said, examine some of the corporate crisis examples presented above. More importantly, consider our practical solutions on how to deal with them. Not only should you address one, but you should also find ways to prevent a crisis and mitigate its risk.

Ultimately, an inevitable corporate crisis doesn't have to stop your business from growing. Just be prepared.

Chapter 12:
Executive and Employee Compensation

Employee and executive compensation can take many forms, each designed to attract, retain, and motivate talent. The differences primarily stem from the level of responsibility, impact, and performance expectations associated with the roles. Below is a breakdown of **different forms of compensation** and **how they differ between employees and executives**:

◆ 1. Base Salary

- **Employees**: Typically receive a fixed hourly wage or annual salary based on job duties and market rates.
- **Executives**: Usually receive significantly higher salaries, reflecting their strategic role and broader responsibilities.

◆ 2. Bonuses

- **Employees**: May receive performance-based bonuses tied to individual or company goals (e.g., holiday or sales bonuses).
- **Executives**: Often have larger, structured bonus plans based on company financial metrics (e.g., EBITDA, stock price), sometimes with guaranteed minimums.

◆ 3. Commissions

- **Employees**: Common for sales roles; earnings are tied to revenue generation.
- **Executives**: Less common, but may be part of roles like Chief Revenue Officer; commissions are usually structured around high-value deals or targets.

◆ 4. Overtime Pay

- **Employees**: Eligible if classified as non-exempt under labor laws (e.g., Fair Labor Standards Act).
- **Executives**: Generally classified as exempt and not eligible for overtime.

◆ 5. Stock Options / Equity Compensation

- **Employees**: May receive options or restricted stock units (RSUs), particularly in startups or tech firms.
- **Executives**: Often receive a significant portion of compensation in equity (stock options, RSUs, or performance shares) to align their interests with shareholders.

◆ 6. Profit Sharing

- **Employees**: Can receive a percentage of company profits based on tenure or salary.
- **Executives**: Usually have larger profit-sharing agreements, often linked to overall corporate performance.

◆ 7. Deferred Compensation

- **Employees**: Rarely offered except in higher-level or long-tenure roles.
- **Executives**: Common; a portion of income is deferred to a later date, often for tax planning or retention purposes.

◆ 8. Retirement Plans

- **Employees**: Typically have access to 401(k) or similar defined contribution plans with limited employer match.
- **Executives**: May receive supplemental executive retirement plans (SERPs), non-qualified plans, or enhanced contributions.

◆ 9. Perks & Fringe Benefits

- **Employees**:
  - Health insurance
  - Paid time off
  - Education reimbursement
- **Executives**:
  - Company car or car allowance
  - Travel allowances
  - Executive health programs
  - Club memberships

      o   Concierge services

◆ 10. Signing & Retention Bonuses

- **Employees**: Occasionally offered to key technical staff or in high-demand fields.
- **Executives**: Frequently offered as part of hiring packages or to discourage jumping to competitors.

◆ 11. Severance & Golden Parachutes

- **Employees**: Typically limited or none unless negotiated.
- **Executives**: Often included in employment contracts; can be substantial and include cash, benefits, and accelerated vesting of equity.

◆ 12. Incentive Pay

- **Employees**: Tied to specific performance goals, usually in the short term.
- **Executives**: Often tied to multi-year strategic goals, including total shareholder return, revenue growth, or profitability.

◆ Summary: Key Differences

Compensation Element	Employees	Executives
Base Pay	Market-based, fixed	High, strategic premium
Bonuses	Performance or holiday	Large, performance-based
Equity/Options	Rare or limited	Common and substantial
Deferred Compensation	Rare	Often used for tax & retention
Retirement Plans	Basic 401(k)	Enhanced or custom plans
Perks	Standard benefits	Luxurious and tailored
Severance	Limited	Negotiated, often substantial

Here's a breakdown of the **tax treatment** for the various forms of compensation for **employees and executives**, including when taxes are paid, who pays them, and how they are reported.

📑 1. Base Salary & Wages

- **Taxable?** Yes
- **When Taxed?** At the time of payment
- **Tax Type:** Subject to:
  - Federal income tax
  - State and local income tax (where applicable)
  - Social Security (6.2%) & Medicare (1.45%) taxes (FICA)
  - Employer also pays a matching share of FICA

💰 2. Bonuses

- **Taxable?** Yes
- **When Taxed?** When paid
- **Tax Type:**
  - Treated as supplemental wages by the IRS
  - Often subject to flat withholding (currently 22% federal; 37% for bonuses over $1 million)
  - Also subject to FICA and state/local taxes

💼 3. Commissions

- **Taxable?** Yes
- **When Taxed?** When earned/paid
- **Tax Type:** Same as wages (federal/state income, FICA)

⛑ 4. Overtime

- **Taxable?** Yes
- **When Taxed?** With each paycheck
- **Tax Type:** Standard income and payroll tax treatment

5. Stock Options / Equity

◆ Non-Qualified Stock Options (NSOs)

- **When Taxed?** At exercise
- **Tax Treatment:**
  - Ordinary income tax on the difference between the market price and the strike price at exercise
  - Subject to income tax and payroll taxes

◆ Incentive Stock Options (ISOs)

- **When Taxed?** At sale (if holding requirements are met)
- **Tax Treatment:**
  - No regular income tax at exercise
  - May trigger **Alternative Minimum Tax (AMT)**
  - If held long enough, taxed at **long-term capital gains** on sale

◆ Restricted Stock Units (RSUs)

- **When Taxed?** At vesting
- **Tax Treatment:**
  - Ordinary income tax on the market value at vesting
  - Subject to FICA
  - Reported on W-2

6. Profit Sharing

- **Taxable?** Yes
- **When Taxed?**
  - If paid in cash: taxable in the year received
  - If deferred into a retirement account, taxed when withdrawn
- **Tax Treatment:** Same as wages (if paid now), or deferred if routed into a qualified plan like a 401(k)

⬇ 7. Deferred Compensation

- **Taxable?** Yes
- **When Taxed?** When received (not when earned)
- **Tax Treatment:**
  - Subject to income tax when the money is paid out (often during retirement, at a lower tax rate)
  - Must comply with IRS **Section 409A** rules to avoid penalties

---

🏠 8. Retirement Plans

◆ 401(k), 403(b), etc.

- **Taxable?**
  - Contributions: Pre-tax (reduces current taxable income)
  - Growth: Tax-deferred
  - Withdrawals: Taxed as ordinary income

◆ Roth 401(k)

- **Contributions:** After-tax
- **Withdrawals:** Tax-free (if qualified)

◆ Non-Qualified Plans (for executives)

- No immediate deduction to the employer
- Taxed to employee upon receipt (not deferral)
- Subject to Section 409A

🎁 9. Perks & Fringe Benefits

- **Taxable?** Depends on the benefit

Perk	Taxable?	Notes
Health Insurance	No	Exempt from income and payroll taxes
Group Term Life Insurance	Partially	First $50,000 excluded; remainder is taxable
Company Car (personal use)	Yes	Taxable fringe benefit
Executive Health Physicals	Often yes	If not medically necessary
Club Memberships	Usually yes	Unless business use can be proven

⚙ 10. Signing / Retention Bonuses

- **Taxable?** Yes
- **When Taxed?** When paid
- **Tax Type:** Same as regular or supplemental wages (22% or 37% flat rate withholding + FICA)

♟ 11. Severance / Golden Parachutes

- **Taxable?** Yes
- **When Taxed?** When paid
- **Tax Type:**
  - Subject to income tax and FICA
  - **Golden parachutes** (large severance after change of control): If they exceed certain thresholds, they are subject to a **20% excise tax** under **IRC Section 280G**

☐ Summary Table

Compensation Type	Taxable?	When Taxed	Tax Type
Base Salary	Yes	When paid	Income + FICA
Bonus (Cash)	Yes	When paid	Income + FICA (22%/37%)
Commissions	Yes	When paid	Income + FICA
Overtime Pay	Yes	When paid	Income + FICA
Non-Qualified Stock Options (NSO)	Yes	At exercise	Income + FICA
Incentive Stock Options (ISO)	Conditional	At sale	Capital gains or AMT
Restricted Stock Units (RSUs)	Yes	At vesting	Income + FICA
Profit Sharing (Cash)	Yes	When received	Income + FICA
Profit Sharing (Deferred)	Deferred	When withdrawn	Ordinary income
Deferred Compensation	Deferred	When received	Ordinary income (409A)
401(k) Plan (Traditional)	Deferred	At withdrawal	Ordinary income
Roth 401(k)	No	Qualified withdrawal	Tax-free
Health Insurance	No	N/A	Tax-exempt

Company Car (Personal Use)	**Yes**	**When received**	**Taxable fringe**
Executive Physicals	**Yes**	**When received**	**Taxable fringe**
Golden Parachute	**Yes**	**When paid**	**Income + FICA + Excise (280G)**

Chapter 13:
Drugs and Alcohol in the Workplace

Drug and alcohol misuse in the workplace has far-reaching consequences that ripple across individuals, families, companies, and society. Below is a comprehensive breakdown of the **impacts on various dimensions**:

---

1. Effects on Workers

a. Physical and Mental Health

- **Increased risk of injury** due to impaired judgment, coordination, or reaction times.
- **Mental health disorders** such as anxiety, depression, and paranoia.
- **Higher rates of absenteeism** and tardiness.
- **Poor decision-making** and lack of focus.

b. Job Performance

- **Decline in productivity** and work quality.
- **Frequent mistakes** or errors in tasks.
- **Unreliable behavior**, including missed deadlines or erratic performance.
- **Disciplinary actions** and risk of termination.

---

2. Effects on Companies

a. Financial Costs

- **Lost productivity**: According to the National Safety Council, substance use costs U.S. employers over **$80 billion annually**.
- **Increased insurance premiums** (workers' comp, liability, health).
- **Costs for accidents** and equipment damage.
- **Recruitment and training expenses** due to turnover.
- **Legal liabilities**: especially if incidents occur on-site or during work hours.

b. Safety Concerns

- **Workplace accidents**: Impaired employees are more likely to be involved in accidents, especially in high-risk industries (e.g., construction, transportation).
- **Endangerment of co-workers**, clients, or the public.
- **Regulatory violations**: Breaching OSHA, DOT, or other agency rules.

c. Organizational Culture

- **Lower employee morale**: Non-using employees may feel unsafe or overburdened.
- **Increased conflict**: Poor behavior, harassment, or aggression.
- **Damage to reputation**: A company known for tolerating substance abuse may lose credibility.

3. Effects on Families

a. Emotional Strain

- Increased **stress, anxiety, and emotional trauma** from a loved one's addiction.
- **Marital problems** or relationship breakdowns.
- **Neglect or abuse of children** in extreme cases.

b. Financial Burden

- Loss of income due to job loss or legal problems.
- **Medical and rehab costs**.
- Potential **homelessness or instability** in severe cases.

4. Financial Ramifications

a. For the Worker

- Loss of wages due to suspension, termination, or time off for rehab.
- **Legal fees**, fines, or imprisonment (e.g., DUIs).
- **Loss of benefits**, insurance coverage, or retirement contributions.

b. For the Employer

- Increased **workers' compensation claims**.
- **Higher healthcare costs**: Employees with substance use disorders cost nearly **twice as much** in healthcare as their peers.
- **Potential lawsuits** from injured employees or third parties.

5. Health Ramifications

a. Short-Term

- Impaired motor functions.
- Poor concentration.
- Fatigue and drowsiness.
- Sudden mood swings or aggression.

b. Long-Term

- **Liver damage**, heart disease, and neurological impairment.
- Development of **mental health disorders**.
- **Addiction-related illnesses** such as Hepatitis or HIV (from injection use).
- Increased risk of suicide or overdose death.

---

6. Business Production Ramifications

- **Disruptions in workflow** due to absenteeism or unreliable performance.
- **Decreased output quality**, missed quotas, or deadlines.
- **Team inefficiencies**: One impaired member can slow down an entire team.
- **Higher staff turnover**, lower long-term team cohesion.
- **Resource strain**: Supervisors spending more time monitoring or managing impaired staff.

---

7. Legal and Compliance Risks

- **OSHA violations** for unsafe work environments.
- **DOT compliance failure** in transportation industries.
- **Employment law violations**: Wrongful terminations or failure to accommodate.
- **Civil liability**: If an impaired worker harms a customer or co-worker.

---

8. Prevention and Mitigation Strategies

- **Drug-Free Workplace Policies** with clear consequences.
- **Employee Assistance Programs (EAPs)** that offer confidential counseling and referrals.
- **Random drug testing** (when legal and appropriate).
- **Supervisor training** to recognize signs of impairment.
- **Wellness programs** focused on mental health and stress management.

- ## Summary Table

Impact Area	Key Consequences
Workers	Injuries, illness, absenteeism, poor performance
Companies	Financial loss, liability, reputation damage
Families	Emotional trauma, financial hardship
Financial	Lost income, rehab/legal costs, insurance spikes
Health	Addiction, mental illness, chronic disease
Production	Reduced efficiency, missed deadlines, turnover
Legal	OSHA violations, lawsuits, DOT fines

WORKPLACE SUBSTANCE ABUSE POLICY TEMPLATE

Purpose:
To provide a safe, healthy, and productive workplace by preventing accidents and injuries resulting from substance abuse.

Scope:
This policy applies to all employees, contractors, and visitors of [Company Name].

Policy Statement:
[Company Name] maintains a zero-tolerance policy towards the use, possession, distribution, or sale of illegal drugs or alcohol during work hours, on company premises, or while conducting company business.

Prohibited Conduct:
- Use, possession, sale, or distribution of illegal drugs or alcohol.
- Reporting to work under the influence of drugs or alcohol.
- Refusal to submit to testing when there is reasonable suspicion.
- Tampering with a drug or alcohol test.

Testing Procedures:
Testing may occur under the following conditions:
- Pre-employment screening
- Random testing
- Post-accident testing

- Reasonable suspicion

Assistance:
Employees struggling with substance abuse are encouraged to seek help through the Employee Assistance Program (EAP).

Disciplinary Actions:
Violations of this policy may result in disciplinary action, up to and including termination of employment.

Acknowledgment:
All employees must sign an acknowledgment form indicating they have read and understood this policy.

⊘ Drug & Alcohol-Free Workplace ⊘

"Your Safety. Your Future. Our Responsibility."

At [Company Name], we are committed to maintaining a safe, healthy, and productive environment for everyone.

Substance abuse puts lives at risk, reduces productivity, and affects morale. To protect our team and uphold our standards, our workplace is strictly:
✓ Drug-Free
✓ Alcohol-Free
✓ Safety-Focused

We Support Our Employees:
• Access to confidential Employee Assistance Programs (EAP)
• Wellness and rehabilitation resources
• Supervisor training and awareness programs

If you or someone you know is struggling, help is available.

Together, we can maintain a workplace that is safe, respectful, and thriving.

Report concerns confidentially to HR or your Supervisor | We're Here to Help

Chapter 14:
Profit Acceleration Tools & Software
(QuickBooks, CRMs, automation, AI for small biz)

Artificial Intelligence Technologies and Tools are available now to smaller companies... they offer to automate, optimize, and enhance operations, customer service, marketing, and decision-making—without requiring large budgets or technical teams. It allows small businesses to **compete more efficiently**, make smarter decisions, and offer better customer experience.

🔍 How AI Benefits Small Businesses

Area	AI Application	Benefits
Customer Service	Chatbots, virtual assistants	24/7 support, quick response, reduced labor
Marketing	Email personalization, social media insights, AI-generated content	Higher engagement, better ROI, time savings
Sales	Predictive analytics, lead scoring, CRM automation	Better conversions, targeted outreach
Operations	Inventory management, logistics, scheduling	Reduced waste, optimized supply chain
Finance	AI bookkeeping, fraud detection, automated invoicing	Accuracy, reduced accounting costs
HR	Resume screening, interview scheduling, employee sentiment analysis	Faster hiring, better retention
Security	AI threat detection, anomaly monitoring	Stronger cybersecurity at lower cost

🛠 Common AI Tools for Small Business

Here are some affordable, user-friendly tools:

Category	Tool	Use
Customer Service	Zendesk AI, Tidio, Intercom	Chatbots, helpdesk automation
Marketing	Mailchimp, Jasper, Copy.ai, HubSpot	Campaign optimization, content creation
Sales	Salesforce AI, Zoho CRM, Gong.io	Lead analysis, voice transcription
Finance	QuickBooks with AI, Xero, Melio	Expense tracking, invoicing
HR & Hiring	BambooHR, Breezy HR, HireVue	AI resume filters, HR automation

Category	Tool	Use
Scheduling	Calendly, Clara, x.ai	Smart scheduling and calendar management
Cybersecurity	Avast AI, Norton, CrowdStrike Falcon	Threat prevention and system scanning

⚙ How Small Businesses Can Get Started with AI

1. **Identify repetitive tasks** that can be automated (e.g., customer FAQs).
2. **Select cloud-based tools**—no infrastructure or tech staff needed.
3. **Start small**—one department or process at a time.
4. **Use free trials** to test AI tools before investing.
5. **Train staff** and integrate tools with existing workflows.

🚀 Examples of AI in Action

- A **retail store** uses AI to manage inventory and predict customer trends.
- A **consulting firm** uses an AI chatbot to qualify leads and set appointments.
- A **construction company** uses AI to analyze project timelines and flag risk delays.
- A **restaurant** uses AI to analyze customer feedback and adjust menus.

Chapter 15:
Company Team Building: An Integrated Approach

1. 🔧 Defining Roles and Responsibilities

- **Foundational Step**: Begin with a clear definition of every role necessary to meet your business objectives.
- **Key Components**:
  - **Job Title**
  - **Department**
  - **Primary Duties**
  - **Reporting Lines**
  - **KPIs or Success Metrics**

💡 *Tip*: Use job descriptions not just for hiring, but for performance management and training alignment.

2. 👥 Hiring Strategy

- **Types of Hires**:
  - **Full-time Employees**: Ideal for core, long-term roles.
  - **Part-time Employees**: Useful for flexible or seasonal needs.
  - **Interns/Trainees**: Good for pipeline development or temporary support.
- **Hiring Process**:
  1. **Job Analysis & Description**
  2. **Posting & Sourcing**
  3. **Screening & Interviews**
  4. **Selection & Offer**
  5. **Onboarding**
- **Tools**:
  - LinkedIn, Indeed, ZipRecruiter
  - ATS (Applicant Tracking Systems) like Breezy HR, Greenhouse

3. 🌐 Outsourcing: Freelancers & Consultants

- **Freelancers**: Individuals hired for specific tasks (e.g., graphic design, social media).
- **Consultants**: Experts brought in for strategic planning or specialized projects (e.g., HR audits, IT systems).

Best Use Cases:

Freelancer	Consultant
Design, copywriting, admin tasks	Strategy, compliance, operations
Short-term/one-off work	High-value external advisory

✘ *Platforms*: Upwork, Fiverr, Toptal (freelancers); Clarity.fm, GLG, Catalant (consultants)

---

4. 📠 Organizational Charts (Org Charts)

- **Purpose**:
    - ○ Visualize the company structure
    - ○ Clarify reporting relationships
    - ○ Aid communication and growth planning
- **Types**:
    - ○ **Hierarchical**: Traditional pyramid structure
    - ○ **Flat**: Fewer management layers
    - ○ **Matrix**: Dual reporting, often for project-based firms
    - ○ **Functional**: Based on departments (e.g., sales, HR, ops)

Tools: Lucidchart, Canva, OrgWeaver, Microsoft Visio

---

5. 🔄 Employee Lifecycle Management

The **employee lifecycle** refers to the stages an employee experiences within your company:

Stage	Actions
Attraction	Employer branding, recruitment marketing
Recruitment	Job postings, interviews, onboarding
Development	Training, mentorship, growth plans
Retention	Culture, engagement, recognition
Separation	Exit interviews, offboarding, alumni networking

Each stage should be tracked with KPIs like time-to-fill, retention rate, training ROI, etc.

---

6. 🗄 Team Structuring Based on Business Size

Stage	Recommended Structure
Startup (1–5 employees)	Founders multitask; consider outsourcing specialists
Growth (5–20 employees)	Define roles in sales, admin, marketing, and ops
Scale (20–50 employees)	Add mid-level management, HR, finance, IT, legal
Expansion (50+ employees)	Full departments with layered management

7. 🔍 Legal & Financial Considerations

- **Employee vs Contractor**: Misclassification can lead to legal penalties.
- **IP & NDA Agreements**: Especially important with consultants/freelancers.
- **Payroll & Taxes**: Must be handled properly per employment classification.

📊 Sample Org Chart: Small Business (15 Employees)

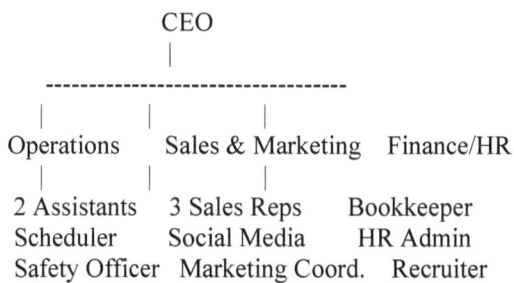

```
                 CEO
                  |
    ----------------------------------
    |            |           |
Operations   Sales & Marketing   Finance/HR
    |            |           |
2 Assistants  3 Sales Reps   Bookkeeper
Scheduler     Social Media    HR Admin
Safety Officer Marketing Coord.  Recruiter
```

✅ Final Tips for Building a Strong Team

- Hire slow, fire fast.
- Document roles, responsibilities, and workflows.
- Use a mix of in-house and outsourced talent for flexibility.
- Conduct regular team reviews and pulse checks.
- Build culture intentionally from day one.

Chapter 16:
Customer Acquisition and Retention: Building Customer Loyalty and Word of Mouth

Customer Acquisition and Retention, with a focus on **Building Customer Loyalty** and **Generating Word of Mouth** — key pillars for long-term business success.

I. Customer Acquisition: Getting New Customers in the Door

Acquisition is the process of attracting and converting prospects into paying customers. It's usually more expensive than retention, s*o it must be efficient and strategic.*

A. Key Strategies for Acquisition

1. **Targeted Marketing**
   - Use demographic, psychographic, and behavioral segmentation.
   - Leverage digital ads, social media, influencer campaigns, and SEO.
2. **Lead Generation & Funnels**
   - Create compelling lead magnets (free guides, trials, webinars).
   - Utilize email nurture sequences to move prospects along the funnel.
3. **Value Proposition & Brand Story**
   - Clearly communicate what makes your product or service better/different.
   - Emotional storytelling helps customers connect with your brand.
4. **Referral Incentives**
   - Offer rewards for existing customers who refer new business.
   - Gamify referrals to increase participation.
5. **Partnerships & Joint Ventures**
   - Collaborate with non-competing businesses that share your audience.
6. **Strong First Impressions**
   - Optimize onboarding.
   - Ensure customer touchpoints (website, packaging, support) reflect quality and clarity.

II. Customer Retention: Keeping the Customers You Acquire

Retention is about delivering consistent value and service to encourage repeat business and reduce churn.

A. Key Retention Strategies

1. **Exceptional Customer Service**
   - Train staff to be helpful, empathetic, and responsive.
   - Implement multichannel support (chat, phone, email).
2. **Consistent Communication**
   - Stay top of mind via newsletters, exclusive offers, tips, and check-ins.
   - Use CRM tools to personalize communication based on behavior.
3. **Customer Feedback Loops**
   - Regularly gather feedback via surveys or reviews.
   - Show customers you're listening by implementing improvements.
4. **Loyalty Programs**
   - Reward repeat purchases with points, tiers, and perks.
   - Surprise customers with unexpected gifts or upgrades.
5. **Product/Service Evolution**
   - Continually innovate based on customer needs.
   - Make customers feel like part of the journey (beta testers, early access).

III. Building Customer Loyalty

Customer loyalty is emotional and behavioral. Loyal customers:

- Spend more overtime.
- Are less price-sensitive.
- Promote your brand willingly.

A. Core Elements of Loyalty

1. **Trust & Reliability**
   - Deliver on promises consistently.
   - Avoid overpromising and underdelivering.
2. **Emotional Engagement**
   - Make customers feel valued and understood.
   - Use personalization and shared values.
3. **Community Building**
   - Create forums, clubs, or online groups.
   - Host events or webinars where customers can connect.
4. **Brand Experience**
   - Ensure every touchpoint (online, offline, support, post-sale) is frictionless and positive.

IV. Word of Mouth: The Most Powerful and Cost-Effective Marketing

Word of mouth (WOM) is when customers voluntarily talk about your brand. It's driven by **delight** and **emotion**, not incentives alone.

A. How to Spark Word of Mouth

1. **Exceed Expectations**
   o Wow customers with unexpected value.
   o Go the extra mile during service delivery.
2. **Create "Talk Triggers"**
   o Unique packaging, fun experiences, shareable stories.
   o Example: Chewy's handwritten pet condolence letters or Zappos' overnight delivery surprise.
3. **Encourage Reviews & Testimonials**
   o Make it easy to review and share feedback.
   o Showcase testimonials and case studies.
4. **User-Generated Content (UGC)**
   o Create hashtags or contests to encourage sharing.
   o Feature customer content on your platforms.
5. **Influencer and Advocate Strategy**
   o Identify micro-influencers or superfans.
   o Give them sneak peeks, insider access, and swag to share.

V. Measuring Success

Use metrics to track the effectiveness of acquisition, retention, loyalty, and WOM:

Area	Key Metrics
Acquisition	CAC (Customer Acquisition Cost), Conversion Rate, CTR
Retention	Churn Rate, Repeat Purchase Rate, CLV (Customer Lifetime Value)
Loyalty	Net Promoter Score (NPS), Loyalty Program Participation
Word of Mouth	Referrals, Social Shares, Review Volume & Sentiment

---

VI. Real-World Examples

- **Apple**: Retains users through ecosystem lock-in, sleek UX, and loyalty programs like iCloud.
- **Starbucks**: Combines mobile convenience, personalized offers, and rewards to retain customers.
- **Tesla**: Created massive word-of-mouth buzz through innovation, a charismatic founder, and customer evangelism.

VII. Final Thoughts

Customer acquisition may get you off the ground, but retention and loyalty are what build lasting, profitable businesses. Word of mouth is the reward for doing both exceptionally well.

💡 **Pro Tip:** Loyal customers become brand ambassadors — and in today's digital world, a satisfied customer with a smartphone is more influential than any billboard.

Chapter 17:
Building Your Business Infrastructure

Types of Training & Who Pays for It
(OSHA, Certifications, CEUs, Cross-Training) **Personal Protective Equipment (PPE)**
(Whose job is it to pay and track usage?)

I. TYPES OF TRAINING

1. Regulatory Training (OSHA, EPA, HIPAA, DOT)

- **Purpose**: Compliance with federal, state, or local laws.
- **Examples**:
    o OSHA 10/30-Hour (Construction/General Industry)
    o HAZWOPER (Hazardous Waste Operations)
    o DOT Hazmat (Trucking & Logistics)
    o HIPAA (Healthcare)
- **Who Pays?**
    o **Employer** is typically required to pay under OSHA's General Duty Clause.
    o Includes time spent in training and materials.

---

2. Certification & Licensing Training

- **Purpose**: Legal/industry qualifications for specialized roles.
- **Examples**:
    o Forklift Operator License (Logistics/Warehouse)
    o Scaffold User & Installer (Construction)
    o First Aid/CPR/AED (All industries)
    o Medical Billing Certification (Healthcare)
    o CDL (Commercial Driver's License)
- **Who Pays?**
    o **Employer** if required for current job role.
    o **Employee** if pursuing independently or for advancement.

---

3. CEUs – Continuing Education Units

- **Purpose**: Maintain credentials for licensed professionals.
- **Examples**:

- o Nurses, Architects, Engineers, Educators
- o Safety Professionals (CSP, CHST, etc.)
- **Who Pays?**
  - o **Split**: Often paid by employers, but can be required by the professional for license renewal.
  - o Some employers reimburse upon successful completion.

---

4. Job-Specific Technical Training

- **Purpose**: Skill development for tools, software, or machinery.
- **Examples**:
  - o CNC Machine Operation
  - o Software platforms (Salesforce, AutoCAD, QuickBooks)
- **Who Pays?**
  - o Usually **employer** as part of onboarding or upskilling.

---

5. Cross-Training & Multi-Skilling

- **Purpose**: Increase workforce flexibility and reduce downtime.
- **Examples**:
  - o Teaching a warehouse worker about inventory software.
  - o Training a medical assistant to handle front desk duties.
- **Who Pays?**
  - o **Employer**, seen as an investment in productivity.

---

6. Soft Skills / Leadership Training

- **Purpose**: Improve communication, leadership, and teamwork.
- **Examples**:
  - o Time management, DEI training, supervisor development.
- **Who Pays?**
  - o **Employer**, especially in large companies or unions.

II. PPE (Personal Protective Equipment)

1. OSHA's General Rule (29 CFR 1910.132)

"Employers must provide PPE at no cost to employees when used to comply with OSHA standards."

---

2. Types of PPE by Industry

Industry	Common PPE	Employer Pays?	Training Required?
Construction	Hard hats, safety glasses, gloves, fall harnesses	✅ Yes	✅ Yes
Medical	Gloves, masks, gowns, eye protection	✅ Yes	✅ Yes (Infection Control, Bloodborne Pathogens)
Logistics	Safety vests, steel-toe boots*, back supports	✅ Yes (vests) / ⊘* (boots usually not covered)	✅ Yes
Manufacturing	Respirators, face shields, earplugs	✅ Yes	✅ Yes (Fit tests for respirators)
Food Service	Gloves, aprons, hairnets	✅ Yes	✅ Yes (Sanitation & Cross-Contamination)

---

3. Exceptions – What Employers Do NOT Have to Pay For

- **Non-specialty safety shoes/boots** (if used off the job site)
- **Everyday clothing** (jeans, long sleeves)
- **Prescription safety eyewear** (if not used exclusively for work)
- **Upgrades requested by employee** (e.g., premium helmet)

▶ But if PPE is required for safety and not optional, the **employer must pay and train.**

III. Who Pays for Training – Summary Matrix

Training Type	Employer Pays?	Employee Pays?	Notes
OSHA/Compliance	✅ Required	⊘	Must be done on company time
Certifications (Job Role)	✅ Often	⊘ or Partial	If certification is required for the role
Certifications (Career Growth)	⊘ Sometimes	✅ Often	E.g., employee seeks a management role
CEUs for Licensing	✅ Sometimes	✅ Sometimes	Shared responsibility

Training Type	Employer Pays?	Employee Pays?	Notes
Equipment/Machine Training	✓ Yes	⊘	Often done during onboarding
Cross-Training	✓ Yes	⊘	Improves internal flexibility
Soft Skills & Leadership	✓ Yes	⊘	Used for career development
PPE	✓ Yes (mostly)	⊘ or partial	OSHA mandates employer to cover job-required PPE

IV. Industry-Specific Requirements

🔧 Construction

- OSHA 10/30
- Scaffold, Fall Protection, Confined Space
- PPE required by law
- Employers must document all training

✚ Medical/Healthcare

- HIPAA, Infection Control, CPR/BLS
- Continuing education mandatory for nurses
- PPE is essential and tightly regulated

🚚 Logistics/Warehouse

- Forklift, DOT Hazmat, Defensive Driving
- PPE includes hi-vis gear, gloves, steel-toe boots
- Training may vary for temp vs. full-time

🏭 Manufacturing

- Lockout/Tagout, Respirator Fit Testing, Machine Safety
- High use of PPE: respirators, gloves, face shields

V. Final Thoughts & Tips for Entrepreneurs

- **Include Training Costs** in your business budget and employee onboarding plans.
- **Document Everything** — it's required for OSHA audits and liability protection.
- **Leverage Grants & Tax Credits** — many states offer workforce development funding.

- **Build a Training Culture** — investing in education builds loyalty, reduces turnover, and creates safer workplaces.

Chapter 18:
Leadership vs. Management

(CEO Mindset, Vision Casting, Motivation, Delegation)

I. Leadership vs. Management – Key Differences

Trait/Focus	Leadership	Management
Mindset	Strategic, visionary, forward-thinking	Tactical, operational, structured
Goal	Inspire change, create direction	Maintain stability, optimize systems
Focus	People and vision	Processes and performance
Time Horizon	Long-term	Short-to-mid-term
Risk	Embraces calculated risk	Minimizes risk
Change	Drives innovation and disruption	Implements and enforces change
Influence Style	Inspiration and empowerment	Authority and supervision
Decision Basis	Vision and values	Policies, KPIs, and results

✓ **Both are essential** — leadership **drives** the organization forward, management **keeps it running.**

II. CEO Mindset – Thinking Like a Leader

1. **Visionary Thinking**
   o Focus on where the company is going, not just where it is.
   o Create a future worth pursuing and articulate it clearly.
2. **Risk Management**
   o Take calculated risks for innovation, while protecting downside.
3. **Decisiveness**
   o CEOs must make tough calls quickly, based on available information.
4. **High Emotional Intelligence (EQ)**
   o Read the room, inspire under pressure, handle conflict gracefully.
5. **Ownership & Accountability**
   o The buck stops here. Own outcomes, good or bad.

III. Vision Casting – Painting the Big Picture

"If you want to build a ship, don't drum up people to gather wood. Instead, teach them to long for the endless immensity of the sea." – Antoine de Saint-Exupéry

Steps to Vision Casting:

1. **Clarify the Destination**
   - Where are we going? Why does it matter?
2. **Align with Values**
   - Ensure vision supports company values and mission.
3. **Communicate It Repeatedly**
   - Use stories, metaphors, and examples to bring it to life.
4. **Connect Emotionally**
   - Show how the vision benefits employees, customers, and the world.
5. **Translate Vision Into Action**
   - Break down big goals into clear, achievable steps.

IV. Motivation – Fueling the Team

A. Types of Motivation

- **Intrinsic**: Purpose, autonomy, mastery
- **Extrinsic**: Pay, perks, promotions

B. Motivational Strategies

- Recognize and celebrate wins
- Connect individual roles to a larger mission
- Provide career growth and learning
- Foster a sense of belonging and psychological safety

V. Delegation – The Art of Multiplication

A. Why Delegation Matters

- Leaders don't scale without it.
- It develops team capacity and frees leaders to focus on strategy.

B. Effective Delegation Process

1. **Define the Task & Objective**
2. **Choose the Right Person**
3. **Give Authority, Not Just Tasks**
4. **Set Deadlines & Checkpoints**
5. **Review and Give Feedback**

⊘ Micromanagement is the opposite of leadership. Trust, then verify.

Chapter 19:
🔒 Security & Data Protection

I. Why It Matters

- Data is a business asset.
- Breaches lead to legal, financial, and reputational damage.
- Compliance is required by law in most industries (GDPR, HIPAA, etc.)

II. Types of Data at Risk

Data Type	Examples
Customer Data	Names, addresses, payment info
Employee Data	Social security numbers, HR records
Financial Data	Bank accounts, invoices
Intellectual Property	Trade secrets, designs, code
Health Data	Medical records, test results

III. Best Practices for Security

A. Technical Safeguards

- **Firewalls & Antivirus Software**
- **Encryption** (in transit & at rest)
- **Multi-Factor Authentication (MFA)**
- **Regular Backups**
- **Secure Wi-Fi & VPNs**

B. Administrative Controls

- Access control policies (least privilege)
- Background checks for sensitive positions
- Written security policies and employee training
- Incident response plans

C. Physical Security

- Lockable file cabinets
- Badge-only access to offices
- Surveillance cameras

IV. Industry-Specific Examples

Industry	Key Requirements & Standards
Medical	HIPAA (Health data privacy), EHR security
Finance	PCI-DSS (Payment info), SOX compliance
Retail/E-Commerce	PCI, GDPR (EU customers)
Construction	Equipment, blueprints, job site access
Logistics	Shipment tracking, customer addresses

V. Who Is Responsible?

- **Owners/Executives**: Ultimate responsibility for data policies.
- **IT & Security Teams**: Implement protections and monitor threats.
- **Employees**: Must be trained in phishing, password hygiene, and safe practices.

⚠ One untrained employee can be the weak link in a $1M firewall system.

VI. Regulations & Compliance

Law/Standard	Applies To	Key Focus
HIPAA	Healthcare	Patient data privacy
GDPR	Any business with EU users	Consent, access, right to be forgotten
PCI-DSS	Any business processing cards	Credit card data security
SOX	Public companies (U.S.)	Financial data protection
NY SHIELD Act	NY businesses handling personal data	Breach notification & security

---

VII. Final Tips

- **Conduct annual security audits**
- **Train all employees regularly**

- **Update software and passwords frequently**
- **Insure against cyber risks** (cyber liability insurance)

Chapter 20:
💼 Record-Keeping & Retention Requirements

(IRS, OSHA, HR, Corporate Governance — Timelines & Responsibilities)

Maintaining proper records is essential for **legal compliance**, **audit readiness**, **risk mitigation**, and **effective business governance**.

I. Why Record-Keeping Matters

- ☐ **Compliance** with federal, state, and local laws
- 🔍 **Audit trail** for financial, tax, or legal scrutiny
- ⚖️ **Evidence** in case of disputes, lawsuits, or claims
- 📈 **Strategic review** and performance tracking

II. General Record Categories

Category	Examples
Financial/Tax	Invoices, receipts, payroll, 1099s, returns
Employment/HR	I-9s, resumes, performance reviews, W-4s
Legal/Governance	Minutes, bylaws, ownership docs, contracts
Safety/Compliance	OSHA logs, incident reports, training records
Operational	Licenses, insurance, permits, client records

III. Record Retention Timelines by Authority

📄 1. IRS / Tax Records

Record Type	Retention Period
Tax returns & supporting docs	**7 years** (minimum)
Payroll tax records (W-2, 941, 940)	**4 years**
Business expense receipts	**7 years**
Depreciation schedules	**Life of asset + 7 years**
1099s, contractor payments	**7 years**

111

🏰 Tip: Keep **longer** if fraud, omitted income, or deductions are in question.

⚠ 2. OSHA (Occupational Safety and Health Administration)

Record Type	Retention Period
OSHA 300, 300A, 301 logs	**5 years**
Safety training records	**At least 3 years**
Medical surveillance (regulated substances)	**Duration of employment + 30 years**
Exposure records (to toxins, noise, etc.)	**30 years**

📟 Special rules apply to construction, maritime, and medical industries.

👔 3. HR / Employee Records

Record Type	Retention Period
Resumes, applications (not hired)	**1 year**
I-9 Forms (Immigration)	**3 years after hire** or **1 year after termination**, whichever is later
Personnel files (current employees)	**While employed + 7 years**
Terminated employee records	**7 years**
Timecards, schedules, payroll	**3–4 years**
Benefits, retirement plan info	**6 years (ERISA)**
Discrimination or harassment claims	**Permanent or until case closes + 3–5 years**

✅ Always document actions related to hiring, discipline, promotions, or terminations.

🏛 4. Corporate Governance & Legal

Record Type	Retention Period
Articles of Incorporation	**Permanent**
Bylaws and amendments	**Permanent**
Board meeting minutes	**Permanent**
Shareholder agreements	**Permanent**

Record Type	Retention Period
Business licenses, permits	**Until expired + 3–7 years**
Contracts (after termination)	**7 years**
Litigation and legal documents	**Until case closes + 7 years**

📁 Keep all **corporate records in an official Corporate Minute Book** or digital equivalent.

IV. Best Practices for Record Retention

1. **Centralized Filing System**
   - Physical or digital (cloud-based secure storage)
   - Clear indexing (by category, year, department)
2. **Retention Schedule**
   - Documented policy for each department
   - Automatic deletion/archive dates for digital systems
3. **Data Security & Privacy**
   - Lock physical files
   - Encrypt sensitive digital records
   - Limit access to authorized personnel
4. **Backups**
   - Maintain regular backups of financial and legal records
   - Test restoration procedures periodically
5. **Compliance Officer or Admin**
   - Assign responsibility for enforcement
   - Conduct regular audits

V. Penalties for Poor Record-Keeping

Type of Non-Compliance	Possible Consequences
IRS audit failures	Fines, interest, disallowed deductions
OSHA violations	Penalties up to $15,625 per violation
EEOC/Fair Labor issues	Discrimination lawsuits, back pay, fines
Corporate disputes	Inability to prove ownership, contracts void
Legal liability	Weak defense in lawsuits
Destruction of records	Criminal Charges

VI. Retention Policy Sample Statement

"**[Company Name] maintains all records in compliance with applicable federal, state, and industry-specific requirements. Records are stored securely, reviewed annually, and destroyed in accordance with regulatory guidelines and internal policies.**"

VII. Final Tips

- ✓ Retain records **digitally AND physically** where possible.
- ✓ Use **cloud platforms** with version control (e.g., Google Workspace, Dropbox Business, SharePoint).
- ✓ Review retention laws in your **specific state/industry**.
- ✓ Include record-keeping policies in **employee handbooks and corporate bylaws**.

Notable **U.S. cases** where an individual was **sentenced to prison for failing to keep—or falsifying—corporate records**:

Case Study: *United States v. K. Kevin James* (2022)

- **Facts of the Case**
  K. Kevin James, a Kansas businessman and co-owner of KC United LLC (which managed companies including Miller Paving LLC), admitted that between 2008 and 2010, he conspired with his accountant to manipulate his company's financial statements. The falsified records overstated profit to maintain favorable banking and bonding conditions. In doing so, he effectively failed to keep truthful corporate records as required by law.
- **Legal Outcome**
  In January 2022, James pleaded guilty to one count of wire fraud. He was subsequently sentenced in November 2022 to **one year and one day in prison**—a sentence that underscores the serious consequences of corporate record falsification. Department of Justice
- **Key Takeaway**
  This case illustrates that deliberately maintaining inaccurate corporate records to deceive financial institutions is punishable with imprisonment—even if the wrongdoing is internal and not publicly visible.

Additional Context: Broader U.S. Legal Landscape

- **Securities Fraud via Stock-Options Backdating**
  Gregory Reyes, former CEO of Brocade, was convicted in 2007 (and reconvicted in 2010) for falsifying corporate accounting books through backdating stock options. His sentence included **21 months in prison** (first conviction) and **18 months** after retrial, plus a $15 million fine.
- **Failure to Report Product Hazards under CPSA**
  In a more recent development, two corporate executives were sentenced in **June 2025** for failing to report product defects to the Consumer Product Safety Commission (CPSC). They were convicted of conspiracy to defraud and failure to report hazards—violations involving corporate record omission—and received prison terms.

Summary Table

Case / Person	Record Issue	Sentence
K. Kevin James	Falsified corporate financials	1 year + 1 day in prison (2022)
Gregory Reyes	Stock options backdating/books	18–21 months prison + fine
Executives in the CPSA case	Failure to report product hazards	Federal prison terms (2025)

Why It Matters

Failing to maintain accurate corporate records—or intentionally falsifying them—for the sake of financial benefit or regulatory avoidance can lead to criminal charges and imprisonment. These cases reflect enforcement under wire fraud laws, securities laws, and consumer protection statutes.

Case Study 1: Martin Elling — Willful Obstruction via Document Destruction

- **Background:**
  Martin Elling, a former senior partner at McKinsey & Company, pleaded guilty in January 2025 to one count of knowingly destroying records intended to obstruct a Department of Justice investigation involving McKinsey, Purdue Pharma, and the opioid crisis thefederalcriminalattorneys.com+13Department of Justice+13thefederalcriminalattorneys.com+13.
- **Outcome:**
  In May 2025, Elling was sentenced to **six months in prison** for his actions Department of Justice.

- **Significance:**
  This case underscores that even high-ranking professionals may face prison time for intentionally destroying evidence to thwart federal investigations.

Case Study 2: Robert Cessario — Destruction of Evidence in a Major Corruption Case

- **Background:**
  Robert Cessario, an FBI agent, deliberately erased the hard drive from his work laptop to hide exculpatory evidence in the corruption trial of former Arkansas State Senator Jon Woods, David Toback, Attorney At Law+15Wikipedia+15Department of Justice+15.
- **Outcome:**
  In January 2023, Cessario was sentenced to **six months of home confinement** (unmonitored), followed by **three years of probation** and a **$25,000 fine** Wikipedia.
- **Significance:**
  Even law enforcement officials can face legal consequences and significant penalties for destroying records in an attempt to influence legal outcomes.

Legal Context: Federal Statutes on Record Destruction

Two key federal statutes criminalize the destruction of documents with the intent to obstruct investigations:

- **18 U.S.C. § 1519** – Makes it a federal crime to destroy, alter, hide, or falsify records with the specific intent to obstruct a federal investigation (including bankruptcy proceedings), punishable by up to **20 years in prison** Eisner Gorin LLP+15Information Requirements Clearinghouse+15Department of Justice+15Department of JusticeLegal Information Institute+1.
- **18 U.S.C. § 1520** – Requires corporate auditors to retain audit records for five years. Knowingly destroying such records is a crime, also punishable by up to **10 years in prison** Eisner Gorin LLP.

Summary Table

Person / Role	Offense Description	Sentence
Martin Elling	Destroyed DOJ-relevant documents	6 months prison (2025)
Robert Cessario (FBI)	Destroyed evidence via laptop wipe	6 months home confinement + probation (2023)

Person / Role	Offense Description	Sentence
Statutory Penalties	Obstructing justice or tampering with audit records	Up to 20 years (§ 1519), up to 10 years (§ 1520)

Takeaway

U.S. law treats the destruction of business or corporate records as a serious federal offense, particularly when it interferes with government investigations or undermines financial transparency. These cases show that individuals who willfully destroy or conceal evidence—even senior executives or agents—can face swift prosecution and substantial penalties.

Chapter 21:
⏱ Time Management & Productivity Hacks

(Pareto Principle, Eisenhower Matrix, Systems Thinking)

I. The Case for Time Management

Time is your most **limited resource**. You can't buy more of it — you can only optimize how you use it. Effective time management increases:

- Focus 🔍
- Output 📈
- Profitability 💰
- Sanity ☐

II. 1. Pareto Principle (80/20 Rule)

80% of results come from 20% of efforts.

✅ How to Apply:

- Identify your **top 20% tasks** (high value, high ROI).
- Eliminate or delegate the **bottom 80%** (low impact).
- Prioritize **profit-producing** or **strategic** activities.

Activity Type	Example
20% High ROI	Closing deals, product strategy, team leadership
80% Low ROI	Rewriting emails, long meetings, busywork

III. 2. Eisenhower Matrix

"What is important is seldom urgent, and what is urgent is seldom important." – Dwight D. Eisenhower

Urgent / Important?	Action to Take
Urgent + Important	**Do now** (crises, deadlines)

Urgent / Important?	Action to Take
Not Urgent + Important	**Schedule** (strategic work, planning)
Urgent + Not Important	**Delegate** (interruptions, admin tasks)
Not Urgent + Not Important	**Eliminate** (time-wasters, social scrolls)

✅ Keep the focus on **Quadrant II** for long-term success.

IV. 3. Systems Thinking

Don't just manage time — **optimize systems**.

- **Identify Patterns & Bottlenecks**
  (e.g., recurring tasks, email overload, long approvals)
- **Create Repeatable Processes**
  Use checklists, SOPs (Standard Operating Procedures), automation.
- **Leverage Tools**
    o Project mgmt: Asana, Trello, Monday
    o Calendar blocking: Google/Outlook
    o Focus apps: Pomodoro timers, RescueTime
    o Automations: Zapier, IFTTT, AI assistants
- **Batch Tasks**
  Group similar tasks together for momentum (e.g., calls, emails, errands).

V. Other Productivity Hacks

- **Time-block your calendar** by task type or energy level.
- **Set 90-minute sprints** followed by short breaks (ultradian rhythm).
- **Avoid decision fatigue**: Pre-plan meals, clothes, routines.
- **Say NO more often**: Guard your time like gold.

🌐 Staying Ahead of the Curve

(Industry Disruption, Innovation, Global Trends)

I. Why It Matters

If you're not evolving, you're becoming **obsolete**. Staying ahead of the curve helps you:

- Identify opportunities early 🚀
- Avoid being blindsided by change ⚠
- Position as an industry leader 🏆

II. 1. Spotting Industry Disruption

Signs of Imminent Disruption:

- Technology reducing costs or complexity (e.g., AI, blockchain)
- New business models gaining traction (freemium, subscription)
- Regulatory shifts
- Talent migration to new platforms or sectors

Famous Examples:

- Netflix > Blockbuster
- Uber > Taxi industry
- Canva > Graphic design services
- ChatGPT > Traditional copywriting and customer service

III. 2. Innovation Strategies

Innovation isn't just invention — it's iteration, adaptation, and improvement.

A. Types of Innovation

Type	Example
Product	Apple iPhone, Tesla battery
Process	Toyota Lean Manufacturing
Business Model	Airbnb (asset-light model)
Customer Experience	Starbucks (3rd place atmosphere)

B. How to Build an Innovation Culture

- Encourage calculated risk-taking

- Create idea submission channels
- Reward experimentation, not just success
- Cross-train teams across departments

IV. 3. Tracking Global Trends

A. Key Areas to Watch

- **Technology**: AI, quantum computing, robotics
- **Workforce**: Remote work, gig economy, Gen Z values
- **Sustainability**: ESG, green energy, circular economy
- **Geopolitical**: Supply chain shifts, BRICS growth, sanctions
- **Consumer Behavior**: Personalization, instant delivery, ethical consumption

B. Where to Track Trends

- Industry-specific newsletters (e.g., CB Insights, Gartner)
- Conferences & trade shows
- Global reports (e.g., McKinsey, World Economic Forum)
- Podcasts, TED Talks, LinkedIn Thinkfluencers

V. Proactive Habits of "Ahead of the Curve" Leaders

- Block time each week for **learning** (reading, podcasts, industry updates)
- Attend at least **one conference per year**
- Encourage **reverse mentorship** (young team members teaching execs)
- Benchmark your company against **adjacent industries**

VI. Final Words of Wisdom

"Skate to where the puck is going, not where it has been." — Wayne Gretzky

Being productive is about **doing the right things**.
Staying ahead is about **knowing which things will matter tomorrow**.

Chapter 22:
🛒 E-Commerce & Online Business Expansion

(Platforms, Drop shipping, Digital Products, Customer Service)

I. Why E-Commerce?

- 🌏 Global reach (24/7 sales)
- 🥷 Lower overhead than brick-and-mortar
- ☐ Easily scalable and automatable
- 📈 Access to real-time analytics and customer data

E-commerce is no longer optional — it's a necessity for growth and competitive relevance in nearly every industry.

II. E-Commerce Platforms Overview

Platform	Best For	Notes
Shopify	Physical product stores	All-in-one, beginner-friendly, scalable
WooCommerce	WordPress users	Open-source, customizable, requires hosting
BigCommerce	Medium to large brands	More built-in features than Shopify
Etsy	Handmade, crafts, vintage	Great for solopreneurs and artists
Amazon	Broad market, fast scale	High traffic, but competitive & fee-heavy
eBay	Auctions or secondhand goods	Trusted marketplace, strong international reach
Kajabi/Teachable	Digital courses, coaching	For selling knowledge products and memberships

✅ Choose your platform based on your **business model, product type, and tech comfort level.**

III. Popular E-Commerce Models

A. 1. Inventory-Based Retail

- Buy bulk inventory

- Store in a warehouse or 3PL (Third Party Logistics)
- Control over branding & fulfillment

B. 2. Drop shipping

You sell it. A supplier ships it.

- **Pros**: Low startup cost, no inventory management
- **Cons**: Thin margins, shipping delays, less control over quality
- **Top Suppliers**: AliExpress, Oberlo, Spocket, Printful

C. 3. Digital Products

- No shipping, infinite inventory, high margins
- Examples:
  - E-books, online courses, templates
  - Software, stock photos, music files

D. 4. Print-on-Demand

- Sell custom-designed items (shirts, mugs, posters)
- Partner with providers like Printful, Printify, Gooten

IV. Online Customer Service – A Competitive Edge

A. Why It Matters

- 80% of consumers say experience is as important as product
- Fast support builds trust, reduces returns, and drives repeat business

B. Support Channels

Channel	Best Use Case
Live Chat	Real-time help, sales conversion tool
Email	Common for support tickets, follow-ups
Phone	Ideal for complex issues
Self-Serve FAQ	Saves time, reduces inquiries
Catbots	Automate FAQs, available 24/7

C. Best Practices

- Use customer names & personalize responses

- Offer clear return/refund policies
- Use CRM tools (Zendesk, Gorgias, Freshdesk)
- Automate with helpdesk triggers & canned responses
- Ask for feedback after resolving issues

☞ A fast response time (under 1 hour) boosts conversions dramatically.

V. Key Tools & Integrations for E-Commerce Success

Category	Tools/Apps
Email Marketing	Klaviyo, Mailchimp, ConvertKit
Analytics	Google Analytics, Hotjar, Shopify Reports
SEO/Marketing	Yoast, Ahrefs, SEMrush
Payment Gateways	Stripe, PayPal, Square
Shipping & Fulfillment	ShipStation, Easyship, Pirate Ship
Product Reviews	Yotpo, Judge.me
Upselling/Cross-sell	ReConvert, Bold Upsell

VI. Scaling Strategies for Online Business

1. Email Marketing

- Build segmented lists
- Set up abandoned cart sequences
- Send monthly newsletters and product drops

2. Social Media & Influencers

- Use Instagram, TikTok, and YouTube for product demos
- Partner with micro-influencers for cost-effective exposure

3. SEO & Content Marketing

- Blog regularly using keywords
- Use product pages to answer common buyer questions

4. Paid Ads

- Google Shopping Ads for search intent
- Facebook/Instagram ads for visual discovery
- Retargeting ads to bring visitors back

5. Subscription Models

- Build recurring revenue (e.g., curated boxes, memberships)

6. International Expansion

- Offer multi-currency checkout
- Translate your site for foreign markets

VII. Compliance & Legal Considerations

- Sales tax nexus rules (check your state requirements)
- Privacy policies (especially with GDPR & CCPA)
- Terms of service and return policy pages
- PCI compliance when handling credit cards

VIII. Common E-Commerce Pitfalls (and How to Avoid Them)

Pitfall	Solution
Poor product photos	Use high-resolution, lifestyle shots
Long load times	Optimize images, use fast hosting
Complicated checkout	Minimize steps, offer guest checkout
No customer trust signals	Display reviews, badges, and contact info
Ignoring mobile shoppers	Use responsive design and mobile testing

---

IX. Final Thoughts

E-commerce isn't just a sales channel — it's a business strategy.
The winners are those who combine:
✓ The right products
✓ The right platforms
✓ And a world-class customer experience

Chapter 23:
☸ Business Ethics & Corporate Culture

(Your Code. Your Voice. Your Reputation.)

I. Why Business Ethics Matter

Ethics are not just "good behavior" — they're the **foundation** of trust, sustainability, and long-term success.

A company's ethics guide every decision — from how it treats customers, employees, and vendors, to how it responds in crisis or opportunity.

"Ethics is knowing the difference between what you have a right to do and what is right to do."
— Potter Stewart, U.S. Supreme Court Justice

II. The Three Pillars

👦⚖️ Your Code

Your **core values**, mission, and ethical principles — your "non-negotiables."

- **Examples of Ethical Codes:**
    - Honesty and transparency
    - Fair treatment of employees
    - Environmental responsibility
    - Zero tolerance for discrimination or harassment
    - Commitment to product safety

Build Your Code:

- Create a written **Code of Ethics** or **Code of Conduct**
- Embed it in onboarding, training, and decision-making
- Ensure leadership models the code consistently

🗣 Your Voice

Your voice is how your ethics and culture show up in the real world — in branding, customer service, and crisis response.

- Be **consistent** in tone, messaging, and values across channels.
- Speak **truthfully**, especially when it's difficult.
- Advocate for causes that **align with your mission** (but avoid virtue signaling).

Your brand is not just what you say — it's what you *do* and what others say about you when you're not in the room.

🌐 Your Reputation

Reputation is your most valuable intangible asset. It builds over the **years** and can be destroyed in **minutes**.

- **Built through:** integrity, transparency, consistency
- **Damaged by:** scandals, hypocrisy, poor treatment of stakeholders
- **Repaired by:** ownership, apology, corrective action

💡 Tip: Reputation management starts **internally**. A toxic workplace will eventually leak out into public view.

III. Building a Strong Corporate Culture

A. What Is Corporate Culture?

The collective **attitudes, behaviors, traditions, and values** shared by your team — "how we do things here."

B. Cultural Foundations

- Leadership behavior (walk the talk)
- Workplace policies & rituals
- Hiring and firing practices
- Recognition systems
- Communication style

C. Types of Corporate Culture

Type	Traits	Watch Out For...
Innovative	Risk-taking, creative, fast-paced	Burnout, lack of structure
Collaborative	Team-focused, transparent	Groupthink, decision delays
Performance-Driven	Metrics-based, competitive	Cutthroat behavior, morale issues
Customer-Centric	Empathy, responsiveness, service	Neglecting internal culture
Traditional/Hierarchical	Stable, policy-heavy	Resistance to change

IV. Practical Ethics in Business Decisions

Situation	Ethical Approach
Cutting costs	Don't compromise safety or fairness
Marketing	Avoid false or misleading claims
Vendor selection	Choose based on merit, not kickbacks
Employee discipline	Apply policies fairly and with documentation
Privacy and data	Be transparent and protective of information
Whistleblowing	Create safe channels and act on reports

✅ Ethics is not just about following the law — it's about doing what's right, even when no one's watching.

V. Ethical Leadership: Model from the Top

Leaders **set the tone**. Culture follows example, not memos.

Traits of Ethical Leaders:

- Self-awareness and humility
- Fairness and consistency
- Open communication
- Accountability — especially in mistakes

"People don't quit jobs, they quit toxic leaders." – Harvard Business Review

VI. Creating an Ethical Framework

1. **Define Core Values**
   (e.g., Integrity, Respect, Responsibility, Courage, Sustainability)

2. **Document Behavioral Standards**
   (Clear examples of acceptable/unacceptable conduct)
3. **Establish Reporting Channels**
   (Anonymous hotlines, HR contacts, open-door policies)
4. **Train Regularly**
   (Annual workshops, onboarding ethics modules)
5. **Measure and Improve**
   (Surveys, audits, feedback mechanisms)

VII. When Ethics Are Tested

Crisis reveals culture.

Ask these questions:

- **Is this decision legal?**
- **Is it aligned with our values?**
- **Would I be proud if this were publicized?**
- **Who does this help? Who might it harm?**

VIII. The ROI of Ethics

Outcome	Benefit
Employee trust	Higher retention, engagement
Customer loyalty	Stronger LTV, referrals
Investor confidence	Better funding and valuation
Regulatory protection	Fewer fines, penalties
Brand equity	Increased goodwill and market value

IX. Final Thoughts

"Culture eats strategy for breakfast." — Peter Drucker

A great strategy with a toxic culture **will fail**.
An ethical, strong culture **can survive anything** — including crisis, competition, and change.

Your code. Your voice. Your reputation.
Build them like your business depends on it — because it does.

Chapter 24:
Intellectual Property Protection: Guarding Your Most Valuable Assets

In the competitive world of entrepreneurship, ideas are currency. The name of your brand, the design of your product, the content you produce, and the secret sauce that makes your business stand out are all intellectual properties (IP). Failure to protect them can mean the difference between scaling your empire and losing it to a copycat.

The Importance of IP Protection

Intellectual Property (IP) refers to intangible creations of the human intellect. These assets often form the backbone of a business's competitive advantage. Without formal protection, your work is exposed to theft, misuse, or imitation—sometimes by larger competitors with more legal power. IP protection secures your rights and enhances your company's value.

Key Benefits of IP Protection:

- Legal ownership and recourse
- Barriers to entry for competitors
- Monetization opportunities (licensing, sale)
- Brand recognition and customer trust
- Investor appeal and valuation

Types of Intellectual Property

1. Trademarks

- **Definition**: Identifies and distinguishes the source of goods or services.
- **Covers**: Brand names, logos, slogans, trade dress.
- **Example**: Nike's "Swoosh" and the phrase "Just Do It."
- **Registration**: USPTO (United States Patent and Trademark Office)
- **Duration**: Renewable indefinitely as long as in use.

2. Copyrights

- **Definition**: Protects original works of authorship.
- **Covers**: Books, manuals, artwork, software code, music.

- **Example**: Software code for a training app.
- **Registration**: U.S. Copyright Office
- **Duration**: Life of the author + 70 years (or 95 years for works-for-hire)

3. Patents

- **Definition**: Grants exclusive rights to inventions.
- **Types**: Utility, design, plant
- **Covers**: Processes, machines, product designs
- **Example**: Dyson's cyclone vacuum technology
- **Registration**: USPTO (requires a rigorous application process)
- **Duration**: 20 years (utility), 15 years (design)

4. Trade Secrets

- **Definition**: Confidential business information providing a competitive edge.
- **Covers**: Formulas, recipes, algorithms, client lists
- **Example**: Coca-Cola's secret formula
- **Registration**: Not registered; protected via confidentiality and contracts
- **Duration**: As long as secrecy is maintained

5. Formulas & Recipes

- Often classified as **trade secrets**, unless patented.
- **Example**: KFC's spice blend, Bush's Baked Beans recipe
- Must be kept confidential with secure processes and employee agreements.

▋ Registering Your IP

Why Register?

- Enhances legal standing in infringement cases
- Enables licensing and franchising
- Boosts company valuation

Where to Register:

- Trademarks & Patents: USPTO (www.uspto.gov)
- Copyrights: U.S. Copyright Office (www.copyright.gov)
- International: WIPO (World Intellectual Property Organization)

Steps to Register:

1. Conduct a clearance search
2. File an application with proper documentation
3. Respond to office actions (if any)
4. Maintain and renew as required

🕵️ Famous IP Infringement Cases

⚡ Apple vs. Samsung

- **Issue**: Infringement on design and utility patents (iPhone look and feel)
- **Result**: Apple awarded over $500 million
- **Lesson**: Protects aesthetic and functional design.

⚡ Mattel vs. MGA (Bratz Dolls)

- **Issue**: Dispute over rights to Bratz created by a former Mattel employee
- **Result**: MGA won; Mattel paid $88.5 million
- **Lesson**: Define IP ownership in employment contracts

⚡ Victoria's Secret vs. Victor's Little Secret

- **Issue**: Alleged trademark dilution
- **Result**: Supreme Court ruled against Victoria's Secret
- **Lesson**: Trademarks require proof of harm

⚡ Coca-Cola Recipe Leak

- **Issue**: Alleged reveal of the Coca-Cola formula in a family scrapbook
- **Result**: No formal claim, but raised major brand protection concerns
- **Lesson**: Trade secrets must be guarded rigorously

⊘ Preventing IP Theft: Best Practices

- Use NDAs (Non-Disclosure Agreements) and Non-Competes
- Clearly define ownership in employee/contractor agreements
- Register trademarks, copyrights, and patents early
- Keep trade secrets physically and digitally secured
- Monitor for IP infringement regularly

- Take legal action promptly when violations are detected

🔎 Sidebar Tip for Entrepreneurs

"Always assume your best ideas will be stolen. Protect them in advance so that when they are, you'll have the law on your side."

Protecting your intellectual property is not just a legal formality; it's a strategic business decision. Whether you're a tech founder, food entrepreneur, or creative professional, securing your IP can mean the difference between building a legacy and losing it before it starts.

Chapter 25:
Government vs. Private Contracting—especially through the lens of WMBE

(Women- and Minority-Owned Business Enterprises)—is a crucial topic for entrepreneurs looking to grow by securing public sector work. Here's a detailed breakdown of the key differences, benefits, and strategies for winning government contracts as a WMBE-certified business:

🔍 1. Government vs. Private Contracting: Key Differences

Feature	Government Contracts	Private Sector Contracts
Procurement Process	Formal, structured (RFPs, RFQs, IFBs)	Informal, relationship-based
Regulations	Highly regulated; compliance-driven (FAR, DFARS)	Fewer regulatory hurdles
Payment Terms	Often net 30–90 days; slower	May be quicker (negotiated)
Transparency	High – public records, open bidding	Low – proprietary or undisclosed
Competition	Often more intense, but small business set-asides	Less intense, but depends on relationships
Certifications Matter	Crucial (e.g., WMBE, 8(a), HUBZone, SDVOSB)	Optional or not considered

✅ 2. Benefits of Government Contracting for WMBEs

- **Set-Asides & Preferences:** Federal, state, and local agencies often reserve a percentage of contracts for WMBEs.
- **Certification Leverage:** Certification gives access to targeted opportunities unavailable to non-certified firms.
- **Stability:** Government contracts tend to be longer-term and less affected by market volatility.
- **Capacity Building:** Agencies offer training, mentorship (e.g., SBA's 8(a) program), and joint venture opportunities.
- **Brand Value:** Being a successful government contractor increases credibility in both sectors.

🏛 3. Certification Options for WMBEs

Federal Level:

- **SBA 8(a) Business Development Program**
- **WOSB/EDWOSB (Women-Owned Small Business / Economically Disadvantaged)**
- **Disadvantaged Business Enterprise (DBE)**
- **HUBZone**
- **Service-Disabled Veteran-Owned Small Business (SDVOSB)**

State/Local Level (varies by jurisdiction):

- **WMBE Certification** (NY, CA, IL, and others have specific programs)
- **MWBE (Minority/Women-Owned Business Enterprise)**
- **SBE (Small Business Enterprise)**

💡 Tip: Some cities like NYC and states like California or Illinois have local goals to award 25%+ of contracts to WMBEs.

📈 4. Strategies for Winning Government Contracts as a WMBE

A. Get Certified

- Register with **SAM.gov** (for federal contracts).
- Apply for **WMBE certifications** at local/state levels (e.g., NYC SBS, NYS Empire State Development).
- Join supplier diversity databases (e.g., NMSDC, WBENC).

B. Target the Right Agencies

- Focus on agencies with strong WMBE goals and spending trends.
- Use databases like:
    - **USAspending.gov**
    - **SAM.gov**
    - **NYC PASSPort**
    - **State procurement portals**

C. Respond to RFPs and RFQs

- Read solicitation documents carefully.
- Highlight past performance and WMBE status.
- Emphasize value, price, and compliance.

D. Network and Partner

- Attend procurement events, matchmakers, and pre-bid meetings.
- Partner with primes as a subcontractor (great entry point).
- Leverage mentor-protégé programs (SBA, DOT, etc.).

E. Stay Compliant

- Maintain your certifications and registrations.
- Be audit-ready and document everything.
- Understand invoicing systems (e.g., Invoice Processing Platform for federal contracts).

💼 5. Case Examples

✅ Success:

- A NYC-based MWBE construction firm landed a $2M parks renovation contract by:
  - Becoming MWBE certified with NYC SBS
  - Attending a pre-bid walkthrough
  - Partnering with a prime contractor needing MWBE participation

✖ Failure:

- A tech firm lost a federal bid because:
  - Their SAM.gov registration had lapsed
  - Their WOSB certification wasn't complete
  - They missed key compliance attachments in the RFP

📑 Resources for WMBEs

- **Small Business Administration (SBA)** – www.sba.gov
- **Minority Business Development Agency (MBDA)** – www.mbda.gov
- **State Procurement Offices**
- **City Agencies (e.g., NYC SBS)** – nyc.gov/sbs
- **PTACs (Procurement Technical Assistance Centers)** – now under APEX Accelerators

---

🔑 Final Tips

- **Be patient** – Contracting success is a long game.

- **Track performance** – Past performance is gold for future bids.
- **Market yourself** – Agencies don't always find you—you must show up and follow up.
- **Stay informed** – Regulations, opportunities, and certifications change often.

Chapter 26:
What's Your Business Personality STYLE?
and Why is it Important for Leaders to Know?

These four personality types work and communicate in very different ways. Learning how to identify and understand personality types based on common personality traits is a key component of effective, practical leadership.

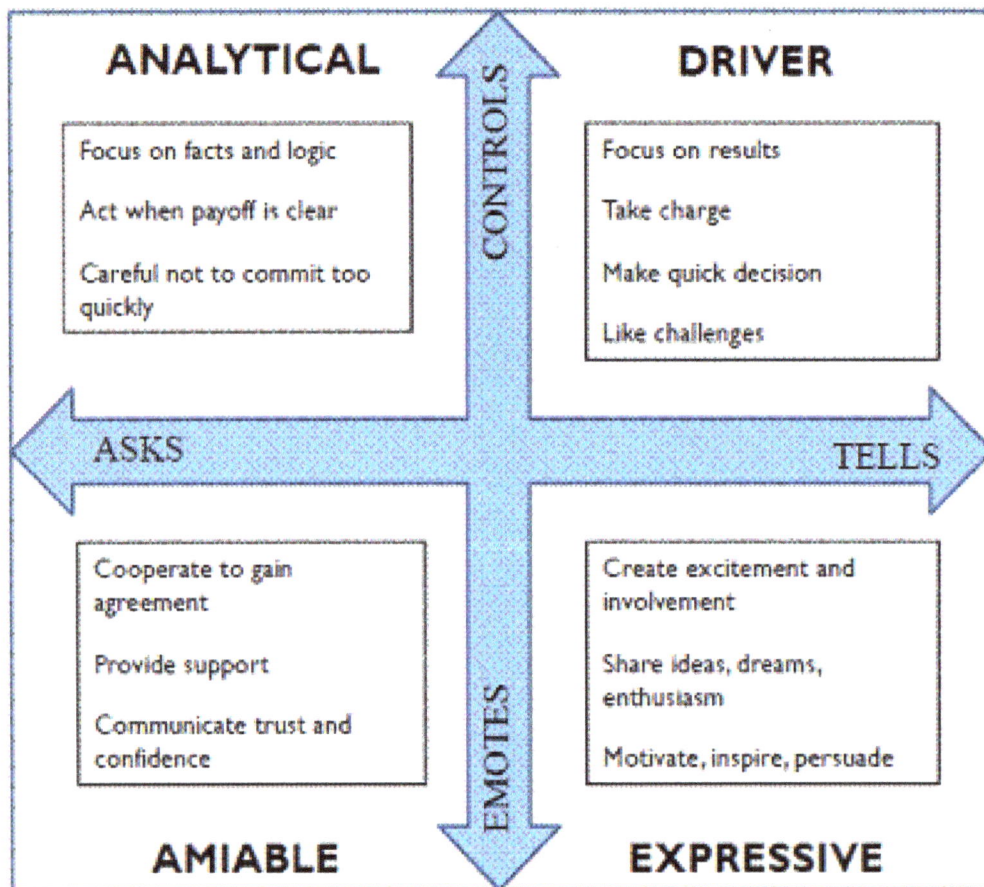

ANALYTICAL

- Focus on facts and logic
- Act when payoff is clear
- Careful not to commit too quickly

DRIVER

- Focus on results
- Take charge
- Make quick decision
- Like challenges

CONTROLS

ASKS — **TELLS**

AMIABLE

- Cooperate to gain agreement
- Provide support
- Communicate trust and confidence

EXPRESSIVE

- Create excitement and involvement
- Share ideas, dreams, enthusiasm
- Motivate, inspire, persuade

EMOTES

The Golden Rule states: *Treat others the way you want to be treated.* While this is generally a good rule of thumb, the reality is that, as leaders, we often must break that rule to relate to the various personality types and manage them effectively. Not everyone in the world communicates and reacts to their environment the same way. Some of us enjoy basking in the glow of the limelight, while others are very uncomfortable with public displays of praise situations.

In my experience, there tend to be four main personality types: analytical, driver, amiable, and expressive. Each personality type exhibits general characteristics, strengths, and weaknesses, and needs to be managed and communicated with in different ways. Understanding these unique traits will help you successfully <u>manage personality types</u> to increase your team's job satisfaction, improve performance, and reach organizational goals.

ADDITIONALY, WHEN IT COMES TO SELLING, REGARDLESS OF THE PRODUCT OR INDUSTRY, YOU NEED TO HAVE THAT BOND OF TRUST WITHIN MINUTES OR YOU WILL LOSE THE SALE.

1. Analytical

The analytical personality type is very deep and thoughtful. Serious and purposeful individuals, analytical types set very high-performance standards, both personally and professionally. They are orderly and organized and tend to have a dry but witty sense of humor.

The strength of analytical personalities lies in their perfectionism, and they want things done right the first time. In addition, analysts are often economical, tidy, and highly self-disciplined. Analytical people's weaknesses are that they can be moody, critical, and negative. As the name implies, they often over-analyze everything and have difficulty making decisions. Their perfectionism is also a weakness at times, as they can be guilty of making their pursuit of perfection stall completion.

2. Driver

Drivers are dynamic and active personality types. They exude confidence and naturally gravitate toward leadership positions. These personalities are goal-oriented but not detail-oriented. Drivers are great with the big picture—they're visionaries and can see how we're going to get to where we need to go. However, drivers are not always great at taking the interim steps necessary to get there.

You can probably see how an analytical type and a driver might not work very well together; however, their skills can nicely complement each other. As one saying goes, if you want to get to the moon, you hire a driver, but if you want to get back, you hire an analytical.

Drivers' strongest characteristic is their determination. They are independent, and they are productive. Drivers are decisive visionaries who get things done. A driver would rather make a bad decision than no decision; they just want a decision to be made.

However, the drivers can also be insensitive, unsympathetic, harsh, proud, and sarcastic. Drivers do not like to admit when they are wrong. They can also rush to a decision without thoroughly thinking through or understanding the results or consequences of their decision.

3. Amiable

First, let's define amiable personalities. Amiable personality types are known for their friendly and pleasant manner. They are typically a patient and well-balanced individual who is quiet but witty. They're very sympathetic, kind, and inoffensive—amiable do not like to offend people. An amiable person is easygoing, and consequently, everybody likes them. Do you know why? Because they don't like conflict, they're very easy to get along with. They're diplomatic and calm. Unfortunately, their weakness is that they can be stubborn and selfish. Amiables' aversion to offense and conflict can make them appear weak or passive.

4. Expressive

We call the expressive social specialist because they love to have fun. They are individuals who turn disaster into humor, prevent dull moments, and are very generous. Expressives want to feel included in everything—projects, teamwork, and conversations.

A great strength of the expressive personality is that they are very outgoing. Likewise, expressive people are ambitious, charismatic, and persuasive. However, they can also be disorganized, undisciplined, loud, and incredibly talkative. Expressives can talk up to 200 words a minute with gusts up to 300. In other words, they can talk!

Of course, these are generalizations, and many people will exhibit some amount of any number of these personality types. However, everyone will more strongly exhibit characteristics of one personality type over all the others. Recognizing and understanding which personality types you manage on your team will help you motivate and communicate with them.

Managing different personality types and personality traits is a difficult part of our roles as managers. However, identifying and understanding how each personality type is motivated and how they communicate is a critical step in effectively managing your team to success.

STYLE Instructions

Understanding Your Style

1. Complete the **Personal Style Inventory on the next page**
2. Tally your **Personal Style Inventory** score
3. Review the result
   - ➢ Do you perceive it as accurate?
   - ➢ What does it mean for you as a member of this team?
   - ➢ Do you recognize these styles in the behavior of others?

Understanding How Others Perceive Your Style

2. Ask two or three other people to complete the **Peer Style Inventory** about you. Print your name at the top of each **Peer Style Inventory**) before distributing.
Examples of whom to ask:
   - ➢ a family member
   - ➢ a past co-worker
   - ➢ a peer or colleague
   - ➢ a direct report (past or present)

Check the word or phrase in each set that is most like you.

1. __ Competitive	1. __ Tries new ideas	1. __ Will power	1. __ Daring
2. __ Joyful	2. __ Optimistic	2. __ Open-minded	2. __ Expressive
3. __ Considerate	3. __ Wants to please	3. __ Cheerful	3. __ Satisfied
4. __ Harmonious	4. __ Respectful	4. __ Obliging	4. __ Diplomatic
1. __ Powerful	1. __ Restless	1. __ Unconquerable	1. __ Self-reliant
2. __ Good mixer	2. __ Popular	2. __ Playful	2. __ Fun-loving
3. __ Easy on others	3. __ Neighborly	3. __ Obedient	3. __ Patient
4. __ Organized	4. __ Abides by rules	4. __ Fussy	4. __ Soft-Spoken
1. __ Bold	1. __ Outspoken	1. __ Brave	1. __ Nervy
2. __ Charming	2. __ Companionable	2. __ Inspiring	2. __ Jovial
3. __ Loyal	3. __ Restrained	3. __ Submissive	3. __ Even-tempered
4. __ Easily led	4. __ Accurate	4. __ Timid	4. __ Precise
1. __ Stubborn	1. __ Decisive	1. __ Positive	1. __ Takes risks
2. __ Attractive	2. __ Talkative	2. __ Trusting	2. __ Warm
3. __ Sweet	3. __ Controlled	3. __ Contented	3. __ Willing to help
4. __ Avoids	4. __ Conventional	4. __ Peaceful	4. __ Not extreme
1. __ Argumentative	1. __ Original	1. __ Determined	1. __ Persistent
2. __ Light-hearted	2. __ Persuasive	2. __ Convincing	2. __ Lively
3. __ Nonchalant	3. __ Gentle	3. __ Good-natured	3. __ Generous
4. __ Adaptable	4. __ Humble	4. __ Cautious	4. __ Well-disciplined
1. __ Forceful	1. __ Assertive	1. __ Aggressive	1. __ Eager
2. __ Admirable	2. __ Confident	2. __ Life-of-the-party	2. __ High-spirited
3. __ Kind	3. __ Sympathetic	3. __ Easily fooled	3. __ Willing
4. __ Non-resisting	4. __ Tolerant	4. __ Uncertain	4. __ Agreeable

TALLYING THE PERSONAL STYLE INVENTORY

Instructions

1. Count the number of "ones" that you marked. Write that number in the Tally Box marked 1. Do the same with the numbers two, three, and four.

2. On the first tally box below, draw a line through the number on the bar graph that corresponds with your total number of "ones." This is the end line for your bar graph.

3. Beginning at the left end, shade the space on the bar up to your end line on the first bar graph.

4. Do the same for the second, third, and fourth graphs.

5. THE LONGEST BAR IS YOUR PREDOMINANT STYLE. THE SECOND LONGEST BAR IS YOUR BACKUP STYLE.

Tally Box

DRIVER

| 1 | | | | 0 1 2 | | 3 4 5 6 | | 7 8 9 10 11 | | 12 14 16 18 |

Expressive

| 2 | | | 0 | 1 2 | | 3 4 5 | | 6 7 8 9 10 | | 11 12 14 16 |

Amiable

| 3 | | | | 0 1 | | 2 3 4 | | 5 6 7 8 9 | | 10 12 14 16 |

Analytic

| 4 | | | 0 1 | | 2 3 4 | | 5 6 7 8 | | 9 10 12 14 |

_____TOTAL (equals 24)

THE DRIVER STYLE: TASK SPECIALIST

THE DOER   *LISTENING*

Growth Action

+ Tends to be perceived as −

Stress Reaction

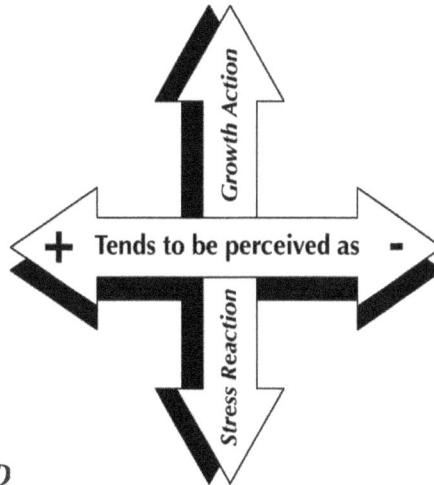

STRONG WILLED   *PUSHY*

INDEPENDENT   *AUTOCRATIC POWER*   *SEVERE*
PRACTICAL   *TOUGH*
DECISIVE   *DOMINATING*
EFFICIENT   *HARSH*

Behaviors

Verbal/Vocal
Faster
More statements
Louder
Monotone
Focuses on task
USES FACTS/DATA

Non-Verbal
Points at others
Leans forward to make a point
Direct eye contact
Closed Hands
Rigid Posture
CONTROLLED FACIAL EXPRESSIONS

Recognized By
Swift reaction time
Maximum effort to control
Minimum concern for caution in relationships
Present time frame
Direct action
Tendency to reject inaction
NEED FOR CONTROL/RESULTS/ACHIEVEMENT

THE ANALYSER: TECHNICAL SPECIALIST

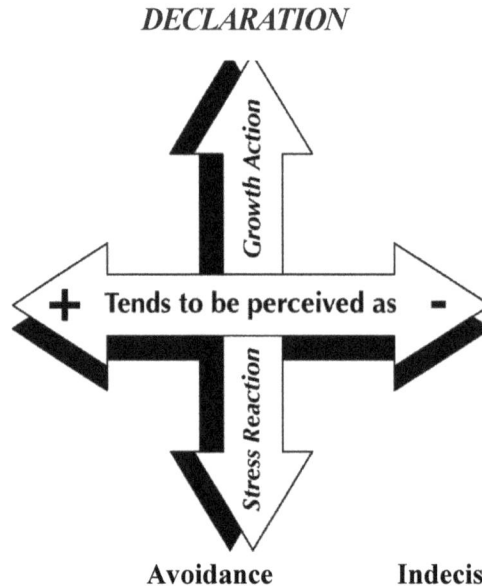

DECLARATION

Growth Action

+ Tends to be perceived as -

Stress Reaction

INDUSTRIOUS		CRITICAL
Persistent	Avoidance	Indecisive
Serious		Stuffy
Exacting		Picky
ORDERLY		MORALISTIC

Behaviors

Verbal/Vocal
Slower
Fewer statements
Softer
Monotone
Focuses on the task
Uses facts/data

Non-Verbal
Slower
Fewer statements
Softer
Monotone
Focuses on the task
Uses facts/data

Recognized By

Slow reaction time
Maximum effort to organize
Minimum concern for relationships
Historical time frame
Cautious action
Tendency to reject involvement
NEED FOR ACCURACY/BEING RIGHT/ACHIEVEMENT

THE EXPRESSIVE STYLE: SOCIAL RECOGNITION SPECIALIST

THE INTUITOR

Checking

Growth Action

+ Tends to be perceived as **-**

Stress Reaction

Personal Attack

Ambitious
Stimulating
Enthusiastic
Dramatic
Friendly

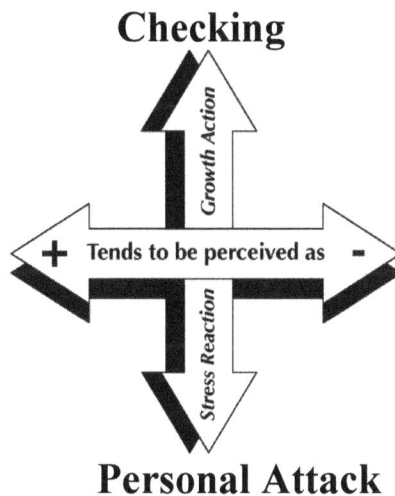

Manipulative
Excitable
Undisciplined
Reacting
Egotistical

Behaviors

Verbal/Vocal	**Non-Verbal**
Faster	Points to others
More statements	Leans forward to make a point
Louder	Direct eye contact
Uses vocal inflection	Open palms
Focuses on people	Casual posture
Uses opinions/stories	Animated expression

Recognized By

Rapid reaction time
Maximum effort to involve
Minimum concern for routine
Future time frame
Impulsive action
Tendency to reject isolation
Need for excitement/personal approach/acceptance

The AMIABLE STYLE: Relationship Specialist

The Feeler

Supportive
Respectful
Willing
Dependable
Agreeable

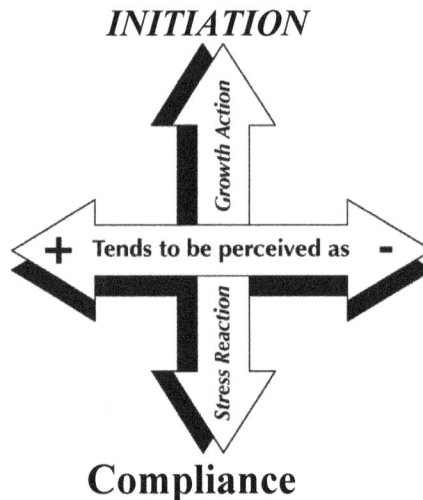

INITIATION

Growth Action

+ Tends to be perceived as -

Stress Reaction

Compliance

Conforming
Unsure
Pliable
Dependent
Awkward

Behaviors

Verbal/Vocal

Slower
Fewer statements
Softer
Uses vocal inflection
Focuses on people
Uses opinions/stories

Non-Verbal

Hands relaxed or cupped
Leans back while talking
Indirect eye contact
Open palms
Casual posture
Animated expression

Recognized by

Unhurried reaction time
Maximum effort to relate
Minimum concern for effecting change
Present time frame
Supportive action
Tendency to reject conflict
Need for cooperation/personal security/acceptance

Assumptions About Personal Styles

There is no best or worst style.
All styles have advantages and disadvantages. All styles are effective when appropriate to the situation and implemented well.

There are no pure styles.
We all have parts of each style in us. However, we also have one style that predominates, one style in which we are most comfortable and which requires the least energy and stress.

Behavior style does not explain the whole person.
It only defines **perceived** patterns of behavior. It does not address personality or an understanding of how an individual thinks or feels.

Much of the population is different from you.
Other people have different needs. Therefore, they communicate in a different manner, use time differently, relate in a different way, make decisions, and manage conflict in a way that differs from how you do it.

We all have goals we hope to attain and results we wish to achieve.
However, different interpersonal priorities influence how we go about accomplishing these ends.

Chapter 27:
Extraordinary Feats Hall of Fame

I CLOSE THIS BOOK BY SHARING EXTRAORDINARY EVENTS BY EXTRAORDINARY LEADERS.

Historic Feats & Remarkable Stories

Apollo 13 – "Failure Is Not an Option"

In April 1970, NASA's Apollo 13 mission suffered a catastrophic oxygen tank explosion en route to the Moon. Against incredible odds, the crew returned safely thanks to ingenuity and teamwork.

1969 – Apollo 11: First Moon Landing

On July 20, 1969, Apollo 11 achieved humanity's first moon landing. Crew: Neil

Armstrong, Buzz Aldrin, Michael Collins.

Descent Drama: Armstrong manually landed the Eagle with less than 30 seconds of fuel to avoid boulders.

Historic Words: "That's one small step for man, one giant leap for mankind."

Legacy: Watched live by over 600 million people, fulfilling President Kennedy's goal and redefining space exploration.

1. **Apollo 13 Launch (April 11, 1970):** The powerful Saturn V rocket lifts off from Kennedy Space Center's Launch Pad 39A, marking the beginning of the ill-fated mission.NASA+10NASA+10The Independent+10NASA+2NASA+2
2. **Crew Portrait (December 1969):** A formal shot of the original prime crew—Commander Jim Lovell, Command Module Pilot Ken Mattingly, and Lunar Module Pilot Fred Haise—captured during pre-flight preparations.NASA+7NASA+7NASA+7
3. **Damaged Service Module:** The Apollo 13 Service Module, seen from the Lunar Module, reveals the devastating effects of the oxygen tank explosion—a panel blown away and fuel cell damage clearly visible.NASA+7Encyclopedia Britannica+7NASA+7
4. **Apollo 13 Mission Patch:** The mission insignia featuring Apollo riding his chariot across the Moon, with the motto *"Ex luna, scientia"* ("From the Moon, knowledge").Wikipedia+1

Context & Additional Visual Highlights

- **Rollout & Launch Imagery:** NASA's archives include numerous photos of the Saturn V rocket during rollout, countdown tests, and various stages leading up to launch.NASA+4NASA+4NASA+4
- **In-Flight & Mission Control Moments:**
  - Dramatic shots from Mission Control during the critical moments following the explosion.NASA+1NASA
  - Interior views of the cramped Lunar Module "Aquarius" used as a lifeboat during the mission.NASA+1
- **Lunar Imagery:** While Apollo 13 didn't land, it provided valuable lunar orbital photography, including farside views of craters like Keeler and Tsiolkovsky—captured as the crew looped around the Moon.NASA
- **Splashdown & Recovery:** Dolby-rich imagery from the mission's dramatic return— featuring the command module's splashdown, crew recovery aboard USS *Iwo Jima*, and the jubilant response by Mission Control.NASA+10NASA+10Space+10

Summary Table

Image/Aspect	Description
Launch Shot	Saturn V liftoff initiating Apollo 13.
Crew Portrait	Lovell, Mattingly, Haise during training — before Swigert replaced Mattingly.
Service Module Damage	Visual confirmation of the explosion's devastating structural impact.
Mission Patch	Iconic emblem symbolizing Apollo 13's legacy.
Control Room & LM Interior	Behind-the-scenes drama from Mission Control and the Lunar Module as a lifeboat.
Splashdown & Recovery	Safe return scenes and NASA's celebratory response.

2009 - The Miracle on the Hudson

In 2009, Captain Chesley Sullenberger safely landed a disabled Airbus A320 on the Hudson River — all 155 aboard survived.

On January 15, 2009, US Airways Flight 1549, piloted by Captain Chesley "Sully" Sullenberger, struck a flock of geese shortly after takeoff from New York's LaGuardia Airport. Both engines failed. With no runway in reach, Sully calmly glided the Airbus A320 and landed it on the Hudson River. All **155 passengers and crew survived** in what became known as "The Miracle on the Hudson." A movie followed

---

1083 - Stanislav Petrov – The Man Who Saved the World

On September 26, 1983, Cold War tensions between the Soviet Union and the United States were at a dangerous peak. Only three weeks earlier, the Soviet military had shot down Korean Air Lines Flight 007, killing all 269 people aboard, including a U.S. congressman. Both nations were on edge, ready to respond to any perceived nuclear strike.

- **Petrov's Role:**
  Stanislav Petrov was a lieutenant colonel in the Soviet Air Defense Forces and was on overnight duty at the *Serpukhov-15* early-warning bunker near Moscow. His job was to monitor satellite systems designed to detect incoming U.S. missiles.
- **The Alarm:**
  Shortly after midnight, the system issued a sudden alert — it reported that **a single intercontinental ballistic missile** had been launched from the United States toward the Soviet Union. Moments later, the system reported **four more missiles** incoming.
- **The Decision:**
  According to Soviet protocol, Petrov's duty was to immediately report the attack as genuine, triggering a retaliatory nuclear strike. This decision had to be made within minutes.
  But something didn't feel right to him:
    o The system reported only a handful of missiles, whereas a real U.S. first strike would likely involve hundreds to overwhelm Soviet defenses.
    o Ground radar did not confirm the satellite data.
    o He knew the satellites were new and could have flaws.
- **His Call:**
  Petrov chose to report it as a **false alarm**, marking it as a "system malfunction" rather than a confirmed launch.
  He later said:
  "I had a funny feeling in my gut. I didn't want to be the one responsible for starting World War III."
- **Aftermath:**
  Investigations revealed the alert was caused by sunlight reflecting off high-altitude clouds, which the satellite's sensors mistakenly read as missile launches.
  Petrov was quietly reprimanded for not filling out his logbook correctly, but he was neither rewarded nor widely recognized at the time. The Soviet military preferred to keep the incident secret.
- **Legacy:**
  Petrov's decision is credited by historians with possibly preventing a nuclear war. His story only became widely known after 1998, when it was declassified.
  He later said he did not see himself as a hero, explaining: *"I was just in the right place at the right time."*

1936 - Hoover Dam Built Ahead of Schedule Engineering Marvel

Completed in 1936, the Hoover Dam was finished two years early despite immense engineering challenges.

When it was completed in 1936, the Hoover Dam was the largest dam and one of the most ambitious engineering projects in history. Built during the Great Depression, it was not just a feat of engineering but also a symbol of hope and progress for America.

Construction Challenges: Located on the Colorado River between Nevada and Arizona, temperatures could reach 120°F (49°C). Workers faced constant risk from falling, drowning, and machinery accidents.

Manpower: More than 21,000 men worked on the project, with a core crew of 5,000.
Innovations: Engineers diverted the Colorado River through massive tunnels and used unprecedented concrete pouring techniques.

1911 - Violet Jessop – The Unsinkable Stewardess

Survived the Olympic collision, Titanic sinking, and Britannic sinking — all major maritime disasters.

Violet Jessop, a stewardess and nurse, survived three maritime disasters.

1911 – RMS Olympic: Collided with HMS Hawke; she survived.

1912 – RMS Titanic: Helped load lifeboats and escaped the sinking.

1916 – HMHS Britannic: Survived a wartime sinking after being pulled underwater by the ship's propellers.

Legacy: Continued working at sea for decades, later publishing memoirs revealing her extraordinary resilience.

1998 - Sara Blakely's $100 Spanx Startup

Torn stockings into a billion-dollar shapewear brand after cold-calling hosiery mills.

Sara Blakely, selling fax machines door-to-door, cut the feet off her pantyhose to improve her outfit's look, sparking a billion-dollar idea.

Starting Out: Invested $5,000 of savings, filed her own patent, and convinced Neiman Marcus to carry Spanx.

Breakthrough: Oprah named Spanx a "Favorite Thing" in 2000, triggering massive sales.

Legacy: Became the world's youngest self-made female billionaire at the time, inspiring countless entrepreneurs.

1944 - The Great Escape Tunnels

In 1944, Allied POWs dug three elaborate escape tunnels using makeshift tools, inspiring the famous film.

In March 1944, Allied POWs in Stalag Luft III executed one of the most daring escape attempts in history.

The Plan: Three tunnels – Tom, Dick, and Harry – were dug 30 feet underground, with ventilation systems and electric lighting.
The Escape: On March 24–25, 76 men escaped through "Harry" before discovery.

1997 - Apple's 90-Day Resurrection

In 1997, Steve Jobs returned to near-bankrupt Apple, streamlined products, and launched the iMac — sparking a global resurgence.

In 1997, Apple was just **90 days from bankruptcy**. Sales were collapsing, product lines were bloated, and Microsoft was dominating the market.

Steve Jobs returned, cut 70% of the products, simplified the lineup, and introduced the iMac — a colorful, internet-ready computer that redefined Apple's image.

By 2001, the iPod and iTunes ecosystem were launched, and the company surged to become one of the most valuable in the world.

2017 - Netflix's Pivot from Mail to Streaming

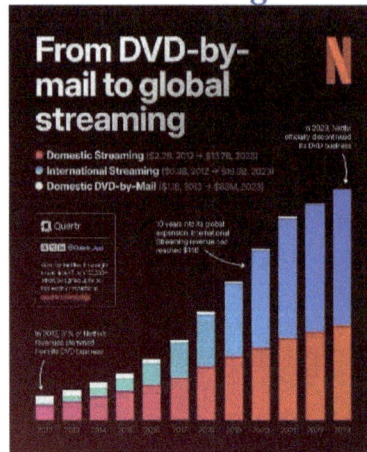

In 2007, Netflix bet on streaming, abandoning its DVD rental business, and ultimately dominating the entertainment industry.

Netflix started in 1997 as a DVD-by-mail rental company, competing with Blockbuster. By 2007, they made the bold decision to **phase out their core business** in favor of streaming — a move that could have destroyed them.
Instead, Netflix became the global streaming leader with over 270 million subscribers, while Blockbuster filed for bankruptcy in 2010.

2003 LEGO's Brick-by-Brick Comeback

In 2003, LEGO refocused on core products and partnerships, transforming into the world's most profitable toy company.

By 2003, LEGO was on the verge of collapse, losing **$300 million a year** due to overexpansion into theme parks, clothing, and electronics.
New CEO Jørgen Vig Knudstorp slashed costs, sold non-core assets, and returned focus to what LEGO did best — **bricks and creativity**.
They partnered with franchises like *Star Wars* and *Harry Potter*, launching record-breaking sets and movies, transforming LEGO into the world's most profitable toy company.

2009 -Domino's Admitting They Weren't Good

In 2009, Domino's openly acknowledged criticism, reinvented its pizza, and grew its stock prices by over 3,000%.

In 2009, Domino's Pizza was facing declining sales and brutal customer reviews — surveys ranked their pizza as **worse than frozen**.
Instead of ignoring criticism, they launched an unprecedented marketing campaign admitting the problem. They completely revamped recipes, added transparency (including live pizza tracking), and aggressively expanded online ordering.
By 2014, stock prices had risen over **3,000%**, making Domino's one of the biggest turnaround stories in the restaurant industry.

2008 - Tesla Betting the Farm

In 2008, Elon Musk invested his last $35 million to save Tesla, later making it the most valuable car company company in the world.

In 2008, Tesla had just weeks of cash left. Elon Musk invested his **last $35 million** to keep the company alive, even as critics doubted electric cars could succeed.
The Model S launch in 2012 stunned the auto industry, earning *Motor Trend's* Car of the Year.
By 2021, Tesla became the world's most valuable carmaker, worth over $1 trillion at its peak.

Legacy: Today, it provides water and hydroelectric power to millions, standing as a testament to early 20th-century ingenuity.

1914 - Ernest Shackleton's Endurance Expedition

In 1914, Sir Ernest Shackleton set out to cross Antarctica, but his ship *Endurance* became trapped and eventually crushed by pack ice. Over the next two years, Shackleton led his crew through extreme cold, hunger, and isolation. Against all odds, **not a single man died**. His leadership and navigation — including an 800-mile journey in a small lifeboat to seek rescue — remain legendary examples of survival and teamwork.

Context & Legacy

- **Photographer Frank Hurley** used heavy glass-plate cameras and was known for his bold methods—he risked life and limb to preserve the visuals, even smashing thousands of negatives to save a few that he carried off the ice. Wikipedia+11Wikipedia+11State Library of New South Wales+11
- **The Expedition's Ordeal**: The *Endurance* became trapped in pack ice and was crushed in October 1915. Shackleton's leadership guided the entire crew of 28 men on an epic journey across ice and sea to safety—marking one of history's greatest survival stories. Amazon+14History Hit+14Reddit+14

- **Modern Discovery**: In 2022, the ship's wreck was discovered in the Weddell Sea, remarkably well preserved nearly 3,000 meters underwater. 3D imagery revealed details like intact woodwork, fittings, and even kitchenware, reaffirming the enduring legacy of Shackleton's expedition. Discover by Silversea+8axios.com+8thesun.

1860 - Nokia's Reinvention

In the 1860s, Nokia began as a **Finnish paper mill**. Over the next century, it transformed itself multiple times — moving into rubber boots, cables, electronics, and finally mobile phones, becoming the world's largest phone manufacturer in the early 2000s. Its ability to reinvent itself across entirely different industries is one of the most remarkable corporate transformations in history.

1885 - Friedrich Trump (later Anglicized to Frederick Trump)

Obstacles He Faced in the Gold Rush Era

1. **Immigrant Hardship**
   - Friedrich Trump emigrated from Kallstadt, Germany, to the United States in 1885 at the age of 16.
   - With little money and limited English, he faced the challenges of integration and finding stable work in an unfamiliar country.
2. **Uncertain Business Ventures**
   - He first worked as a barber in New York before heading west.
   - Like many entrepreneurs during the gold rush, he didn't prospect for gold himself but opened **restaurants and hotels in mining towns**. These ventures were risky—booming only when miners were flush with cash, then collapsing when mines closed or towns declined.
3. **Lawless and Volatile Environments**
   - Mining towns in Washington state, British Columbia, and later in the Yukon during the Klondike Gold Rush were often rough, lawless, and subject to rapid economic swings.
   - Businessmen like Trump had to deal with unreliable supply chains, unpredictable customer bases, and competition from other transient entrepreneurs.
4. **Reputation and Legal Scrutiny**
   - His establishments often included food, liquor, and, according to some historical accounts, sex work. This led to periodic scrutiny from local authorities and difficulties securing long-term legitimacy.
   - For example, when he tried to return to Germany later in life, his reputation and emigration issues (he had left Germany originally to avoid military service) caused problems with German officials, ultimately preventing him from resettling there.
5. **Geographic and Logistical Barriers**

160

    o   Setting up businesses in remote gold rush territories meant transporting goods over long, treacherous routes. In the Klondike, for instance, everything—from lumber to food—had to be hauled by pack animals or riverboats through dangerous terrain.

Summary

Friedrich Trump's path wasn't one of striking gold but of **capitalizing on the miners' needs** in unstable, high-risk boomtowns. His obstacles included immigrant disadvantages, volatile frontier economies, rough social conditions, and later legal challenges both in the U.S. and Germany. Despite this, he managed to accumulate modest wealth, which laid a foundation for the Trump family's later real estate ventures in New York.

Chapter 28:
Most Horrific Company or Individual Events

1. Bhopal Gas Tragedy (1984 – India)

- **What Happened:** A leak of methyl isocyanate gas from Union Carbide's pesticide plant in Bhopal killed over **3,000 people instantly** and caused long-term illness, birth defects, and cancers in over 500,000 residents.
- **Horrific Factor:** Poor maintenance, ignored safety systems, and corporate cover-ups made it the **worst industrial disaster in history**.

2. Enron Scandal (2001 – USA)

- **What Happened:** Enron executives engaged in massive accounting fraud, hiding billions in debt while inflating profits.
- **Impact:** Thousands lost jobs, pensions, and life savings; the scandal destroyed Arthur Andersen, one of the largest auditing firms.
- **Horrific Factor:** A deliberate, calculated deception by top leadership, shattering trust in corporate America.

3. Rana Plaza Collapse (2013 – Bangladesh)

- **What Happened:** A garment factory building collapsed due to ignored structural warnings, killing **1,134 workers** and injuring over 2,500.
- **Horrific Factor:** Workers were forced to return to the building despite visible cracks and evacuation orders.

4. Boeing 737 MAX Crashes (2018 & 2019)

- **What Happened:** Two crashes (Lion Air Flight 610 and Ethiopian Airlines Flight 302) killed **346 people** due to software issues and inadequate pilot training disclosures.
- **Horrific Factor:** Internal documents revealed Boeing prioritized speed to market and cost savings over safety.

5. Theranos Fraud (2003–2018 – USA)

- **What Happened:** Elizabeth Holmes misled investors, doctors, and patients by claiming her company's blood-testing technology could perform hundreds of tests from a single drop of blood.
- **Horrific Factor:** Patients received false results, leading to incorrect diagnoses and treatment.

---

6. Tylenol Cyanide Murders (1982 – USA)

- **What Happened:** Seven people in Chicago died after taking Tylenol capsules laced with cyanide.
- **Horrific Factor:** Caused nationwide panic and changed pharmaceutical packaging forever. The killer was never caught.

---

7. Bernie Madoff Ponzi Scheme (1960–2008 – USA)

- **What Happened:** Madoff ran the largest Ponzi scheme in history, defrauding investors of **$65 billion**.
- **Horrific Factor:** Destroyed charities, ruined retirements, and led to several suicides among victims.

---

8. Ford Pinto Fires (1971–1978 – USA)

- **What Happened:** The Ford Pinto's fuel tank was prone to explosion in rear-end collisions.
- **Horrific Factor:** Internal memos revealed Ford calculated it was cheaper to pay legal settlements for deaths than to fix the design.

---

9. Wells Fargo Fake Accounts Scandal (2002–2016 – USA)

- **What Happened:** Bank employees created millions of unauthorized accounts to meet aggressive sales targets.
- **Horrific Factor:** Customers faced credit damage, fees, and financial harm due to systemic corporate pressure and fraud.

---

10. Challenger Space Shuttle Disaster (1986 – USA)

- **What Happened:** The shuttle exploded 73 seconds after launch, killing all seven crew members, including schoolteacher Christa McAuliffe.
- **Horrific Factor:** NASA managers ignored engineers' warnings about faulty O-ring seals in cold weather.

---

11. Donald Trump Jr. The 1989 Helicopter Crash

What Actually Happened

The 1989 Helicopter Crash

- On **October 10, 1989**, a leased Agusta A109 helicopter crashed into a wooded median along the Garden State Parkway in New Jersey while returning from New York to Atlantic City. All **five people aboard** perished, including **three top executives of the Trump casino operations**:
    - **Stephen F. Hyde**, CEO of Trump Castle and Trump Plaza
    - **Mark Grossinger Etess**, president & COO of the forthcoming Taj Mahal
    - **Jonathan Benanav**, Executive Vice President of Trump Plaza
      ([Los Angeles Times, Oct 11, 1989]UPI+10Los Angeles Times+10nomadicpolitics.blogspot.com+10; [UPI Archives]UPI)

Impact on Trump's Casino Empire

- The crash dealt a severe blow to Trump's Atlantic City operations. Hyde and Etess were critical figures behind the management and promotion of his casino projects—particularly the newly built and expensive **Taj Mahal**, which opened shortly afterward.
- One year later, the Taj Mahal was deeply indebted—nearly **$3 billion**—and Trump's casinos—including the Taj Mahal, Trump Plaza, and Trump Castle—filed for **bankruptcy** in the early 1990s. Trump himself later publicly blamed the catastrophic loss of these executives for contributing to his businesses' financial decline.Reddit+7nomadicpolitics.blogspot.com+7Los Angeles Times+7

The "Narrow Escape" Story

- After the crash, media reports quoted Trump's office saying he had **almost boarded the helicopter** himself but changed plans at the last minute.The Standard+2nomadicpolitics.blogspot.com+2
- However, this was widely challenged—critics and biographers alleged it was a **preemptive PR move** rather than a fact. Trump biographer Harry Hurt described how Trump appeared to be crafting a self-serving narrative immediately after the tragedy. X (formerly Twitter)+4nomadicpolitics.blogspot.com+4nomadicpolitics.blogspot.com+4

Organizational Response

- One of the immediate consequences was the appointment of **Robert Trump** (Donald Trump's brother) to succeed Mark Etess in his role following the crash. Los Angeles Times+3Wikipedia+3X (formerly Twitter)+3

Final Thoughts

- Yes, there was a truly tragic helicopter crash involving **Donald Trump Sr.'s casino executives in 1989**, and it had **significant financial and managerial repercussions** for the Trump Organization's Atlantic City ventures.
- But there is **no record or evidence** that **Donald Trump Jr.** was ever involved in or had any connection to such an event.

---

12. The company was an internet advertising / lead-generation firm called 800xchange (often reported as 800XChange or "The 800 Exchange").

In June 2010, Orange County tech entrepreneur Christopher Ryan Smith vanished; years later, his business partner, Edward Younghoon "Ed" Shin, was tried and, in December 2018, convicted of first-degree murder with a special-circumstance finding of financial gain. He was sentenced to life without parole in July 2019. Smith's remains have never been found.

Most Catastrophic Business Failures

---

1. Enron (2001 – USA)

- **Industry:** Energy, Commodities
- **Collapse Trigger:** Accounting fraud using off-balance-sheet entities to hide debt and inflate profits.
- **Impact:** $74 billion in shareholder value wiped out, thousands lost jobs and pensions, and accounting giant Arthur Andersen was dissolved.
- **Lesson:** Short-term manipulation can destroy even the most admired companies.

---

2. Lehman Brothers (2008 – USA)

- **Industry:** Investment Banking
- **Collapse Trigger:** Excessive exposure to subprime mortgage-backed securities during the U.S. housing bubble.
- **Impact:** $600 billion in assets lost, triggering the global financial crisis.

- **Lesson:** Overleveraging in risky markets without liquidity safeguards is fatal.

---

3. WorldCom (2002 – USA)

- **Industry:** Telecommunications
- **Collapse Trigger:** $11 billion accounting fraud to inflate earnings.
- **Impact:** Largest U.S. bankruptcy at the time, devastating employees, investors, and the telecom sector.
- **Lesson:** Corporate culture without accountability invites massive fraud.

---

4. General Motors Bankruptcy (2009 – USA)

- **Industry:** Automotive
- **Collapse Trigger:** High labor costs, declining market share, and the 2008 financial crisis.
- **Impact:** $82 billion U.S. government bailout, restructuring, and loss of market dominance.
- **Lesson:** Failure to adapt to consumer trends and global competition erodes industry leadership.

---

5. Blockbuster (2010 – USA)

- **Industry:** Video Rental
- **Collapse Trigger:** Ignored the streaming revolution and failed to acquire Netflix for $50 million in 2000.
- **Impact:** From 9,000 stores to one remaining franchise in Bend, Oregon.
- **Lesson:** Disruption can kill even market leaders if they fail to pivot.

---

6. Kodak (2012 Bankruptcy – USA)

- **Industry:** Photography
- **Collapse Trigger:** Invented the digital camera in 1975 but feared cannibalizing its film business.
- **Impact:** Lost its dominant position, filed for bankruptcy after missing the digital wave.
- **Lesson:** Innovation without adaptation is wasted.

---

7. Pan American World Airways (1991 – USA)

- **Industry:** Aviation
- **Collapse Trigger:** Rising fuel costs, increased competition, and the 1988 Lockerbie bombing destroyed brand trust.
- **Impact:** Once the world's most iconic airline, it ceased operations entirely.
- **Lesson:** Brand prestige can't survive sustained financial and reputational crises.

---

8. Theranos (2018 – USA)

- **Industry:** Health Tech
- **Collapse Trigger:** Fraudulent claims about revolutionary blood testing technology.
- **Impact:** Investors lost hundreds of millions; founder Elizabeth Holmes convicted of fraud.
- **Lesson:** Hype without viable technology leads to catastrophic collapse.

---

9. WeWork (2019–2023 – USA)

- **Industry:** Office Space Leasing
- **Collapse Trigger:** Overexpansion, questionable accounting, and leadership scandals.
- **Impact:** Valuation plummeted from $47 billion to bankruptcy.
- **Lesson:** Growth without sustainable business fundamentals is a house of cards.

---

10. Barings Bank (1995 – UK)

- **Industry:** Banking
- **Collapse Trigger:** Unauthorized derivatives trading by rogue trader Nick Leeson.
- **Impact:** A 233-year-old bank bankrupted, bought for £1.
- **Lesson:** Weak internal controls can destroy even the oldest institutions.

Notorious Rogue Employee Incidents

---

1. Nick Leeson – Barings Bank Collapse (1995 – UK)

- **Role:** Derivatives Trader in Singapore.
- **Action:** Hid massive trading losses in a secret account while doubling down to recover them.
- **Impact:** Losses of £827 million bankrupted Barings Bank, a 233-year-old institution.

- **Lesson:** Lack of oversight and separation of duties can be fatal.

---

2. Edward Snowden – NSA Mass Surveillance Leak (2013 – USA)

- **Role:** Contract IT Administrator for the NSA.
- **Action:** Leaked classified documents revealing global surveillance programs.
- **Impact:** International diplomatic crises, exposure of intelligence methods, and major policy debates.
- **Lesson:** Contractors and employees with privileged access can bypass even top-level security if not monitored.

---

3. Chelsea Manning – WikiLeaks Military Leaks (2010 – USA)

- **Role:** U.S. Army intelligence analyst.
- **Action:** Released hundreds of thousands of classified documents, videos, and cables to WikiLeaks.
- **Impact:** Exposed U.S. military operations, caused diplomatic fallout, and endangered informants.
- **Lesson:** Weak insider controls in sensitive systems can lead to global consequences.

---

4. Terry Childs – San Francisco Network Hostage (2008 – USA)

- **Role:** Network Administrator for San Francisco's Department of Technology.
- **Action:** Refused to hand over administrative passwords to the city's FiberWAN network.
- **Impact:** Locked out city officials for 12 days; network access restored only after Childs was jailed.
- **Lesson:** No single employee should hold sole control of mission-critical credentials.

---

5. UBS Trader Kweku Adoboli (2011 – UK)

- **Role:** Trader at UBS Investment Bank.
- **Action:** Unauthorized trades and false accounting to hide losses.
- **Impact:** $2.3 billion loss; UBS's reputation badly damaged.
- **Lesson:** Rogue risk-taking can cripple even major financial institutions.

---

6. Ray Bowen – Home Depot Data Breach (2004 – USA)

- **Role:** IT security contractor.
- **Action:** Stole 13,000 employee payroll records and sold them.
- **Impact:** Data breach lawsuits, internal security overhaul.
- **Lesson:** Vendors can be as risky as full-time staff for insider threats.

7. The Tesla "Sabotage" Case (2018 – USA)

- **Role:** Tesla Gigafactory employee.
- **Action:** Elon Musk accused the employee of altering code in manufacturing systems and leaking sensitive data to outsiders.
- **Impact:** Temporary production disruptions, legal battles.
- **Lesson:** Disgruntled insiders with technical skills can disrupt operations rapidly.

8. Société Générale Trader Jérôme Kerviel (2008 – France)

- **Role:** Trader at Société Générale.
- **Action:** Made massive unauthorized trades totaling €50 billion in exposure.
- **Impact:** €4.9 billion in losses; nearly bankrupted the bank.
- **Lesson:** Rogue trades can bypass detection if risk monitoring systems are poorly enforced.

9. Anthony Levandowski – Google/Waymo Trade Secrets Theft (2016 – USA)

- **Role:** Senior engineer at Google's self-driving car project.
- **Action:** Downloaded thousands of confidential files before leaving to start his own venture with Uber's support.
- **Impact:** Uber settled with Waymo for $245 million; Levandowski was convicted of trade secret theft.
- **Lesson:** High-value intellectual property is prime for insider theft.

10. The Cisco Source Code Leak (2004 – USA)

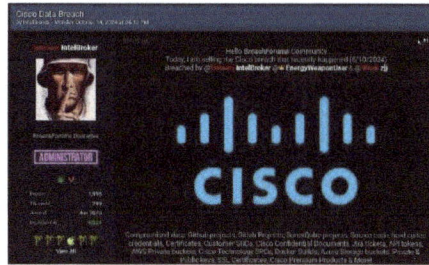

- **Role:** Cisco engineer (name undisclosed).
- **Action:** Leaked proprietary router source code online.
- **Impact:** Security vulnerabilities exposed worldwide; damage to Cisco's market confidence.
- **Lesson:** Software source code is a crown jewel that must be tightly controlled.

11. The Crazy Eddie Scandal: A Retail Empire Fueled by Fraud

Origins & Rise

- Founded in **1969** in Brooklyn as *Sight and Sound*, the store was rebranded **Crazy Eddie** by Eddie Antar and his father, Sam M. Antar—initials forming ERS Electronics YouTube+11Wikipedia+11GAUTFONTs+11.
- By combining **bargain pricing**, aggressive advertising, and flashy commercials (led by Jerry Carroll delivering the memorable slogan *"His prices are ins-a-a-a-ne!"*), The chain expanded rapidly across the New York/New Jersey area ACFE+3Wikipedia+3The New Yorker+3.
- At its peak, Crazy Eddie boasted **43 stores** and over **$300 million** in annual sales YouTube+11Wikipedia+11GAUTFONTs+11.

Fraudulent Business Practices

From day one, the Antar family built the business on illicit foundations:

- **Skimming sales**: They under-reported cash transactions, skimmed tax, and paid employees off the books—often pocketing roughly **$1 out of every $5** in reported income GAUTFONTs+8Wikipedia+8Financial Pipeline+8.
- **Money laundering ("Panama Pump")**: Skimmed funds were physically moved—taped to bodies—to Israel, then routed through Panama banks and reinjected into the company to inflate reported sales Wikipedia+1.
- **Public offering fraud**: Crazy Eddie went public in **September 1984**, inflating profits via skimmed cash, fraudulent inventory counts, and overland to boost valuations and enrich insiders GAUTFONTs+6Wikipedia+6Financial Pipeline+6.
- **Inventory manipulation**: Fraudulent overstatement of inventory—$3 million in 1985, climbing to $10–12 million by the next year—further masked decline, Wikipedia.

Collapse & Legal Fallout

The fraud began to unravel by **1986–1987**:

- Stock value plummeted, Eddie cashed out millions in shares (reportedly worth $25–30 million), and resigned as CEO WikipediaCliffsNotes.
- In late **1987**, new management discovered inventory discrepancies up to **$80 million**, prompting creditors to push Crazy Eddie into bankruptcy. By **1989**, all stores were liquidated CliffsNotes+4Wikipedia+4Financial Pipeline+4.
- Legal probes followed: the **SEC**, **FBI**, and **IRS** launched investigations, supported by insider testimony—particularly from cousin and CFO Sam E. Antar, who had turned state's evidence Nicki Swift+3Wikipedia+3The New Yorker+3.
- Eddie fled to Israel in **1990** under a false identity, was extradited in **1993**, briefly convicted, retried, and ultimately pleaded guilty in **1996**. He was sentenced in **1997** to **eight years in prison**, over **$150 million in fines**, and civil judgments exceeding **$1 billion** Wikipedia.

Aftermath & Legacy

- The Crazy Eddie brand saw multiple failed revival attempts—from a 1998 store in New Jersey and online ventures to later e-commerce relaunches (2001–2005) and more — all short-lived Wikipedia+2Nicki Swift+2.
- Eddie Antar passed away in **2016**, remembered by some as a flamboyant, if fraudulent, New York retail legend New York Post+6Wikipedia+6ACFE+6.
- His story was chronicled in the 2022 book *Retail Gangster* by Gary Weiss, who called Crazy Eddie "the Darth Vader of capitalism" ACFE+3Wikipedia+3Entrepreneur+3.
- The scandal offers enduring lessons in **white-collar crime**—from how cult-like loyalty and deception allow fraud to flourish, to how even sophisticated audits can be fooled by "controlled chaos," as Sam Antar described it CliffsNotes.

What Actually Happened

- **Fled the U.S.**: In February 1990, Eddie Antar fled the United States using a forged Brazilian passport, assuming the alias David Jacob Levi Cohen. He settled in Yavne, Israel, while authorities pursued him Going Concern+7Wikipedia+7lechnerlaw.com+7.
- **How he was found**: Investigators uncovered his location by tracing his monetary transfers from U.S. accounts through Swiss intermediaries. This led to collaboration between the FBI and Israeli law enforcement pacfe.orgWikipedia.
- **Arrest**: In June 1992, Eddie was captured by Israeli police in Yavne, entirely independently of the U.S.Findlaw+3pacfe.org+3Wikipedia+3.
- **Other Antars arrested too**: On the same day, his brothers Mitchell and Allen were arrested as well

---

Quick Summary

Aspect	Details
Founder	Eddie Antar (with Sam M. Antar)
Peak Scale	43 stores, $300M+ sales
Frauds Included	Skimming, money laundering, inventory inflation, false profits
IPO	1984 at $8/share; later manipulated upward
Collapse	Inventory fraud uncovered, bankruptcy in 1989
Conviction	Guilty plea in 1996, sentenced to 8 years + heavy fines
Legacy	Failed revivals, cultural imprint, cautionary tale

Some additional Frauds (closest parallels)

ZZZZ Best (Barry Minkow)

- **Industry**: Carpet-cleaning (but positioned as a nationwide service co.)
- **Fraud**: At age 16, Barry Minkow founded ZZZZ Best and falsely claimed lucrative insurance restoration contracts.

- **Methods**: Created fake contracts, staged buildings, faked revenues, used shell companies.
- **Collapse**: Went public in 1986; by 1987, auditors exposed the fraud, losses over **$100 million**.
- **Aftermath**: Minkow was sentenced to 25 years; later became a pastor, but returned to prison for new frauds in the 2000s.

A Bit of Context

- **What Was ZZZZ Best?**
  Founded by Barry Minkow in the early 1980s, ZZZZ Best started as a legitimate carpet-cleaning business before expanding into insurance restoration, a large portion of which was entirely fabricated. The company became a front for an elaborate Ponzi scheme that eventually collapsed, costing investors and banks around **$100 million**. The fraudulent restoration business accounted for about 86% of the company's revenue. InvestopediaInvestopedia+4Wikipedia+4EBSCO+4
- **The Exposure and Aftermath**
  A disgruntled homemaker who had been overcharged prompted an investigation by *The Los Angeles Times*. That coverage triggered scrutiny, prompting banks to call in loans and investors to rethink their positions. Investigations revealed that purported restoration "sites" were often just mailboxes; auditors had been deceived with fake documents and staged site tours. ZZZZ Best ultimately declared bankruptcy in 1987, and Minkow was indicted in 1988 on multiple charges—including racketeering, securities fraud, and embezzlement—and sentenced to 25 years in prison (though he was released after serving a shorter term).

Comptronix (1990s)

- **Industry**: Computer board manufacturer
- **Fraud**: Top executives inflated revenues by falsifying shipping records and creating phantom inventory, much like Crazy Eddie.
- **Impact**: Investors lost hundreds of millions before discovery.
- **Aftermath**: Executives convicted of securities fraud, wire fraud, and money laundering.

Company Overview

- **Comptronix Corporation** was a publicly traded company (OTC: CMPX) specializing in contract manufacturing of printed circuit boards for electronics, including medical equipment and computer peripherals. The company became known for rapid growth in the late 1980s and early 1990s ssgca.com.
- Founded in 1984, it expanded quickly and employed around 1,700 people by 1993 across multiple locations AAA Publications+2SSRN+2.

Infamous Accounting Fraud

- In the early 1990s, Comptronix executives—including the CEO, COO, and CFO—were implicated in a large-scale accounting fraud. They inflated earnings through improper practices such as overstating inventory, understating costs, and even recording fictitious sales comptronix.cz+8Course Sidekick+8Gale+8.
- The scandal led to financial distress, the eventual sale of its operations in the mid-1990s, and a Chapter 11 bankruptcy filing in 1996 Gale+4ssgca.com+4Course Sidekick+4.

MiniScribe (1989)

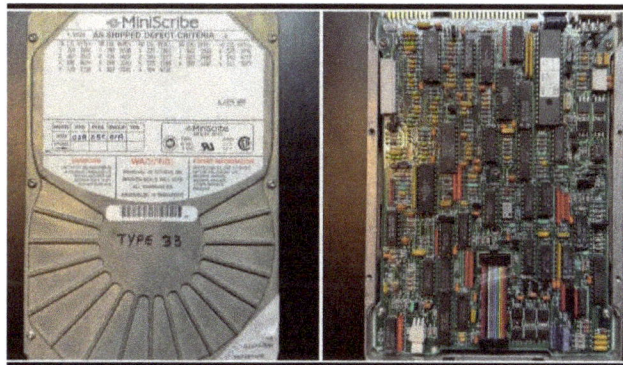

- **Industry**: Hard disk drive maker
- **Fraud**: Executives inflated inventory by literally **shipping boxes of bricks** to distributors and counting them as sales.
- **Collapse**: Losses of $500 million when uncovered; Arthur Andersen, their auditor, was sued.
- **Aftermath**: CEO sentenced to prison; case became a classic in accounting textbooks.
- The **MiniScribe 8051A**, a 42 MB 3.5-inch hard drive, was indeed produced in 1989. It featured an IDE/PATA interface, 3.5" half-height form factor, and detailed internal specifications like cache, tracks, platter count, and more. bugworkshop.blogspot.com+1
- 1989 was also when MiniScribe's inventory fraud scandal came to light. A bizarre and notorious facet of this fraud involved shipping **bricks instead of hard drives**—packaged

in HDD boxes—to inflate inventory counts during audits.
Dreamstime+14StorageNewsletter+14Golang Project Structure+14

An internal evaluation described how senior management orchestrated this scheme to mask financial shortfalls and manipulate sales and inventory reporting. The Washington Post+2latimes.com+2

- MiniScribe's assets were ultimately acquired by Maxtor in 1990 after the company declared bankruptcy

---

🏢 Broader Corporate Accounting Frauds

Enron (2001)

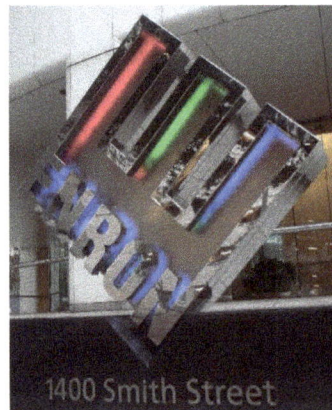

- **Industry**: Energy trading
- **Fraud**: Used shell companies (special purpose entities) to hide billions in debt and inflate profits.
- **Collapse**: Largest bankruptcy in U.S. history at the time, wiping out $74 billion in shareholder value.
- **Aftermath**: Executives Jeff Skilling & Andrew Fastow jailed; Arthur Andersen collapsed after shredding audit docs.
-
- **What Was Enron?**
  Enron Corporation was founded in 1985 via a merger between Houston Natural Gas and InterNorth, evolving into a major energy, commodities, and services company headquartered in Houston, Texas. At its height, the company generated nearly $101 billion in revenue and employed over 20,000 people, Wikipedia+6Wikipedia+6Encyclopedia Britannica+6.
- **The Scandal & Collapse**
  In late 2001, Enron's downfall began when it filed for Chapter 11 bankruptcy—the then-largest such case in U.S. history—triggered by revelations of massive internal accounting fraud. The scandal exposed deceptive practices like off-balance-sheet entities and

mark-to-market accounting, designed to mask debt and inflate earnings Wikipedia+10Wikipedia+10The Enron Saga+10.

- **Legacy & Aftermath**
  The collapse spurred widespread regulatory reform, most notably the passage of the Sarbanes–Oxley Act in 2002, which introduced stricter financial disclosures and accountability for corporate executives WikipediaTIMEEncyclopedia Britannica.
- **Investigations & Fallout**
  The FBI led one of its largest white-collar crime investigations, seizing over 3,000 boxes of documents, collecting terabytes of digital evidence, and helping hold senior Enron executives legally accountable Federal Bureau of Investigation.

WorldCom (2002)

- **Industry**: Telecommunications
- **Fraud**: CEO Bernie Ebbers directed billions in false accounting entries to inflate cash flow and profits.
- **Collapse**: Declared bankruptcy; shareholders lost ~$180 billion.
- **Aftermath**: Ebbers sentenced to 25 years (served 13).

A Brief Recap of the WorldCom Scandal

- **What Happened:** WorldCom, once the second-largest long-distance phone company in the U.S., was found to have engaged in massive accounting fraud between 1999 and 2002. Executives improperly capitalized ordinary expenses as investments and manipulated reserves, ultimately overstating assets by more than **$11 billion** seeklogo.com+13en.wikipedia.org+13www.slideshare.net+13rudfp.weebly.com+1.
- **Discovery & Fallout:** The fraud was uncovered by internal auditors led by Cynthia Cooper, revealing **$3.8 billion** in fraudulent entries, which later totalled much more. This triggered the largest bankruptcy in U.S. history at the time, wiping out thousands of jobs and causing enormous losses for investors en.wikipedia.org+1.

- **Consequences:** CEO **Bernard Ebbers** and CFO **Scott D. Sullivan** were ultimately criminally convicted for their roles. The scandal was a key catalyst for the **Sarbanes–Oxley Act**, which imposed stricter corporate governance and financial accountability measures rudfp.weebly.com+9en.wikipedia.org+9www.slideshare.net+9.

Adelphia Communications (2002)

gettyimages
Credit: Harry Scull Jr.

- **Industry**: Cable TV
- **Fraud**: The Rigas family looted company funds for personal use and hid billions in debt.
- **Collapse**: Declared bankruptcy, wiping out shareholders.
- **Aftermath**: John Rigas sentenced to 15 years; son Timothy to 20.

🔑 Common Threads with Crazy Eddie

- **Inventory manipulation** (Crazy Eddie, Comptronix, MiniScribe)
- **Skimming/cash fraud** (Crazy Eddie, Barry Minkow)
- **IPO/public stock manipulation** (Crazy Eddie, ZZZZ Best, Enron)
- **Family or "tight circle" involvement** (Crazy Eddie's family, Rigas family at Adelphia)
- **Cult of personality** around founders/CEOs to deflect scrutiny

Chapter 29:
Startup Formation & Entrepreneurship Trends

1. Increases in Startup Formation Under Democratic Administrations

- A 2023 study found that startup rates in Democratic counties increased relatively after Barack Obama's election, but declined relative to Republican counties following Donald Trump's election. Specifically, the startup rate rose by **2.3%** of the mean one year after 2008, and by **3.5%** one year after 2016. That corresponds to about **21,000 new firms** after 2008 and **40,000** after 2016. Rady School of Management

2. Partisan Shifts in Entrepreneurship Among Individuals

- Between 2005 and 2017, data from 40 million Americans show that **6% of Republicans** and **4% of Democrats** became entrepreneurs. Moreover, Republicans increased their entrepreneurship during Republican administrations and decreased it during Democratic ones—a shift equal to **170,000 new firms** overall. Marginal REVOLUTION

3. National Small Business and Startup Growth Under Biden (Democratic)

- Since President Biden took office in early 2021, there have been approximately **21 million new business applications**—the **highest total in any U.S. presidential administration**—with an average of **440,000 applications per month**, roughly **90% higher** than pre-pandemic averages. Joint Economic Committee+6Small Business Administration+6Small Business Administration+6
- From 2021 to the first quarter of 2023, the U.S. added **2.8 million new private-sector establishments**, and small businesses added a net **7.2 million jobs**. Small Business Administration
- Even more broadly, between 2019 and 2023, startup counts (firms under 1 year old) grew by **16%**, more than 2.5 times the growth rate of 2015–2019. Most of this surge occurred in 2022 and 2023. Center for American Progress
- Corresponding Treasury data also show **430,000 new business applications per month** in 2024—50% above 2019 levels—while small businesses accounted for **70% of net new jobs** since 2019. U.S. Department of the Treasury+2Reuters+2

Broader Economic Context: Job Creation & Growth

While not solely about startups, broader economic performance under different administrations provides valuable context.

4. Generally Stronger Economic Indicators Under Democratic Presidents

- Since WWII, key economic metrics—like job creation, GDP growth, stock market returns, and personal income growth—have tended to perform better under Democratic administrations. Recessions have also disproportionately started under Republican presidents. The White House+5Wikipedia+5Joint Economic Committee+5
- From Truman through Trump, **Democratic presidents oversaw ~70.5 million jobs created**, versus **29.1 million** under Republicans. That's an average of **164,000 jobs per month** for Democrats, versus **61,000** for Republicans—2.4× higher. Wikipedia+1

5. Annual Growth Differences

- One analysis shows **real GDP growth was 1.2 percentage points faster**, job growth averaged **2.5% annually under Democrats** versus just over **1% under Republicans**, and business investment grew more than twice as fast under Democratic administrations. Reuters+5Economic Policy Institute+5EPI Action+5

6. Jobs Created by Administration (Recent Terms)

- For more granular data: during Obama's two terms, **~11.6 million private-sector jobs** were added (measured from February 2009 to January 2017), which was a record pace. Wikipedia+2Wikipedia+2
- Trump's presidency saw a **net loss** of around **2.7 million jobs**. Joint Economic Committee
- Biden's term (2021–2025*) has seen job growth of **~16.15 million nonfarm employment**, representing an **11.3% increase**. Wikipedia

*As of very recently (data updated through early-2025).

Summary Table

Metric / Trend	Democratic Administrations	Republican Administrations
Startup Formation (county-level)	↑ 2.3–3.5% post-election (21k–40k firms)	Declines relative to Democratic counties
Individual Entrepreneurship Rate	4% overall; decreases during Dem terms	6% overall; increases during GOP terms (170k total)
New Business Applications (Biden Era)	~21M apps; 440k/month, highest on record	Not comparable; significantly lower activity
Jobs Created per Month	~164k jobs (Democratic average)	~61k jobs (Republican average)
Job Growth Rate (Annual)	~2.5%	~1%
Real GDP Growth (Annual)	~3.79%	~2.60%

A Note on Startup Success (Survival Rates)

About startup success specifically—like survival or failure rates under different administrations—but **there's virtually no data linking startup survival to presidential party**.

The broader literature offers general survival statistics (e.g., ~**90% of startups fail within a few years**), but these aren't broken down by administration or party. marketwatch.comRady School of Management+1Small Business Administration+5Marginal REVOLUTION+5marketwatch.com+5abcnews.go.com+3EPI Action+3Marginal REVOLUTION+3Reuters+4Small Business Administration+4Small Business Administration+4Small Business AdministrationWikipedia+7Reuters+7Wikipedia+7

Final Thoughts

- **Formation of startups** appears to be more robust during Democratic administrations, particularly at the county and national levels under Biden.
- **Republican administrations** show stronger individual entrepreneurial activity among Republicans themselves—but not necessarily at the broader startup ecosystem level.
- **Overall economic performance**, including job creation and GDP growth, has consistently trended stronger under Democratic presidents.

Top Startups of 2025

1. Thinking Machines Lab

- Founded in February 2025 by former OpenAI CTO **Mira Murati**, this AI startup attracted an **unprecedented $2 billion in early-stage funding**, securing a **$12 billion valuation** just months after founding. Investors include Andreessen Horowitz, Nvidia, AMD, Cisco, and others. Exceptional Startups+10Forbes+10TechCrunch+10Wikipedia

2. Anysphere (Cursor)

- Developer of the AI-native code editor **Cursor**, Anysphere has soared from launch to **$500 million ARR** within three years, now valued at **$9.9 billion** after a $900 million Series C in 2025.Wikipedia

3. Applied Intuition

- A leader in autonomous vehicle software, Applied Intuition raised $600 million in its Series F round and now holds a **$15 billion valuation**. Wikipedia

4. Glean Technologies

- An enterprise AI-powered search company, Glean reached a valuation above **$7 billion** in 2025, up from $4.6 billion in 2024.eadithbmargarita.pages.dev+5Wikipedia+5Wikipedia+5

5. Cohere

- This Canadian AI startup specializes in large language models for enterprise. After raising $500 million, Cohere is focused on deploying LLMs across finance, healthcare, and public sector industries.Wikipedia+2The Wall Street Journal+2

6. Perplexity AI

- A generative AI conversational search engine with explosive growth—**915% growth in searches**, $915 million in Series C funding, and widespread user traction in 2025.Exploding Topics

7. webAI

- Based in Austin, this startup brings AI inference capabilities directly to devices—no cloud needed—offering secure, cost-effective models for enterprises. Raised **$43 million in Series A**.Startup Savant

8-SONO

- An AI music generation platform that turns text prompts into original songs. Headquartered in Cambridge, Massachusetts, Suno has raised **$125 million Series B**. Startup Savant

9. Flyfin

- An AI-powered tax service for self-employed individuals, combining CPA expertise with automation. Based in Silicon Valley, Flyfin has a **$10 million Series A**. Startup Savant

10. Pixxel

- A US–Indian startup building a constellation of **hyperspectral imaging satellites** for Earth observation. One of India's most well-funded space-tech startups, totaling **$95 million in funding** to date. Wikipedia

---

Why These Startups Stand Out

These companies exemplify the innovation and momentum defining 2025:

- **AI Dominance**: Five on the list (Thinking Machines Lab, Anysphere, Glean, Cohere, Perplexity) are pushing the boundaries of artificial intelligence across sectors, from coding to search to enterprise tools.
- **Breakneck Growth**: Anysphere and Thinking Machines Lab achieved multi-billion valuations in record time—within their first few months or years.
- **Diverse Industries**: Whether it's music generation (Suno), tax automation (Flyfin), or space exploration (Pixxel), this list showcases the breadth of innovation.
- **Strong Funding Signals**: These startups aren't just promising—they have deep VC backing, high valuations, and major scale-up potential.

Summary Table

#	Startup	Sector	Highlight
1	Thinking Machines Lab	Generative AI	$12B valuation shortly after launch
2	Anysphere (Cursor)	AI Coding Tools	$500M ARR, valued at $9.9B
3	Applied Intuition	Autonomous Vehicle Software	$15B valuation post Series F
4	Glean Technologies	Enterprise AI Search	Valued > $7B

#	Startup	Sector	Highlight
5	Cohere	LLMs for Enterprise	$500M raised; expanding in regulated sectors
6	Perplexity AI	AI Search/LLM	Explosive growth, $915M Series C
7	webAI	On-Device AI	$43M Series A; no-cloud AI deployment
8	Suno	AI Music Generation	$125M Series B; creative AI
9	Flyfin	Fintech (AI Tax Service)	$10M Series A; CPA+AI automated tax filing
10	Pixxel	Space-Tech / Earth Observation	$95M raised; building hyperspectral satellite network

Chapter 30:
Major Startup Failures in 2025

1. Canoo (EV Startup)

- **What happened**: Canoo filed for Chapter 7 bankruptcy in Delaware, effectively ceasing operations as of January 17, 2025. The company's debt exceeded its assets—estimated at $126 million vs. liabilities over $164 million—and it struggled to secure additional funding, including federal backing.Exploding Topics+4TechCrunch+4Failory+4The Verge+1
- **Why it matters**: It reflects the harsh reality of capital-intensive industries like EV manufacturing, where even high-profile deals (e.g., with NASA or Walmart) couldn't sustain operations amid funding droughts.

2. Builder.ai (AI App Development)

- **What happened**: Once a Microsoft- and QIA-backed startup, Builder.ai entered insolvency proceedings and filed for bankruptcy in mid-2025. Allegations surfaced that its AI claims were overstated—much of the work was reportedly done by human contractors; financial data may have been inflated.Wikipedia+1
- **Why it matters**: This underscores how inflated valuations and misleading storytelling can unravel even well-backed startups once scrutiny increases.

3. Zeen (Social Media / Creator Economy)

- **What happened**: Zeen, previously known as Landing, shut down operations in July 2025 after raising about $9 million. Despite a Gen-Z audience and rebranding efforts (including a shoppable collage tool), it couldn't scale as a VC-backed venture and decided to close rather than try to become profitable.DemandSage+8LinkedIn+8The Economic Times+8Business Insider
- **Why it matters**: It highlights the difficulty of achieving lasting traction in the crowded creator economy, even with pivot strategies and popular appeal.

4. Apostrophe (Telehealth Skincare)

- **What happened**: Hims & Hers shuttered its skincare arm Apostrophe, with subscriptions ending by March 7, 2025. Customers were redirected to Hims or Hers platforms, and refunds processed accordingly.SFGATE
- **Why it matters**: The closure illustrates how larger companies sometimes consolidate overlapping services to streamline operations, even after an acquisition.

5. Astra (SaaS Startup)

- **What happened**: Astra, backed by Perplexity founder Aravind Srinivas, ceased operations in July 2025 due to irreconcilable co-founder conflicts. CEO Supreet Hegde cited personal disagreements as the primary reason for the shutdown.SFGATE+1The Economic Times
- **Why it matters**: It's a reminder that internal dynamics—especially at the co-founder level—can sink a company just as decisively as market forces.

6. Blueprint (Biotech / Longevity)

- **What happened**: Bryan Johnson announced plans to shut down or sell Blueprint—his age-reversal startup—due to financial losses and a renewed focus on his philosophical movement "Don't Die" rather than commercial ventures. The Times of India
- **Why it matters**: It highlights how shifting personal missions or financial difficulties can derail startups, even when they stem from charismatic founders or high-profile experiments.

7, Quintillion, an Alaska-based broadband startup led by CEO Elizabeth Pierce. The company claimed it was building an undersea fiber-optic cable system stretching across the Arctic — intended to connect Alaska with regions like Japan, the Pacific Northwest, Greenland, Iceland, and even Europe.

However, in 2017-2018, it was revealed that Pierce had **forged contracts** to appear financially viable and attract over $250 million in investments — contracts that were fabricated and never real bloomberg.com+3theverge.com+3adn.com+3. The fraud unraveled when clients disputed invoices, triggering investigations that exposed the deceit. Ultimately, Pierce was **charged with wire fraud**, sentenced to prison, and required to pay restitution cablinginstall.com+1.

Summary Table

Startup	Sector	Fate	Primary Reason(s) for Shutdown
Canoo	Electric Vehicles (EV)	Bankruptcy (Chapter 7)	Cash depletion, unsustainable debts, lack of funding
Builder.ai	AI / App Development	Bankruptcy / Insolvency	Misleading tech claims, financial overstretch
Zeen	Social Media / Creator Tool	Shutdown	Inability to scale, unviable business model
Apostrophe	Telehealth (Skincare)	Discontinued by acquirer	Redundant operations within the parent company
Astra	SaaS	Shutdown	Internal co-founder conflicts

Startup	Sector	Fate	Primary Reason(s) for Shutdown
Blueprint	Biotech / Wellness	Planned sell/shutdown	Financial losses, strategic shift of the founder's priorities

Broader Context & Trends

- **Startup failure remains the norm**: As of mid-2025, around **90% of startups will fail**, and **only 10% succeed long-term**.WikipediaWikipedia+4Wikipedia+4The Verge+4The Economic TimesCB InsightsWikipediaBusiness Insider
- **Top causes of failure**:
  - **Poor product–market fit** ($\approx 34\%$)
  - **Marketing errors** ($\approx 22\%$)
  - **Team issues** ($\approx 18\%$)
  - **Cash flow struggles** ($\approx 16\%$)
  - Other factors include tech flaws ($\approx 6\%$) and legal/operational missteps (~2% each).Failory+3Exploding Topics+3tsttechnology.io+3
- **Recent failure trends**: In the U.S., the number of startup shutdowns climbed by 25.6% in 2024 compared to 2023. 2025 is expected to be similarly harsh. Many failures stem from depleted capital—**60% of startups that fail lack sufficient remaining funds to return to investors**

Chapter 31:
Top Companies Succeeding with Earth-Based Minerals (2025)

1. MP Materials (USA)

- **What they do**: Owns and operates the Mountain Pass rare-earth mine—the only active rare-earth mining and processing site in the U.S. They focus on Neodymium-Praseodymium (NdPr) oxides, essential for motors, wind turbines, and other high-tech applications.Freepik+3pheasantenergy.com+3Google Cloud Storage+3Popular Mechanics+4Wikipedia+4Investing News Network (INN)+4
- **Why they stand out**:
    - Ongoing multi-stage expansions to refine and produce magnets and rare-earth alloys domestically.Wikipedia+2Reuters+2
    - Secured a massive U.S. Department of Defense investment—$400 million plus loans and grants—to scale rare-earth processing and manufacturing.Barron's+2Barron's+2
    - Stocks have soared, with strong analyst ratings and EBITDA projections aiming for up to $650 million by decade's end.Barron's+1

2. Lynas Rare Earths (Australia/Malaysia/USA)

- **What they do**: The largest rare-earth producer outside China, mining at Mt. Weld (Australia), refining in Malaysia, and constructing a new separation plant in Texas.StartUs Insights+15Exoswan Insights+15MINING.COM+15
- **Why they stand out**:
    - Recently became the first producer of heavy rare earths outside China—specifically dysprosium—at its Malaysian facility.Equitymaster+1News.com.au
    - Valued at approximately $7.2 billion, and positioned as a critical non-Chinese supplier for Japan, the U.S., and Europe.News.com.au+1

3. Kenmare Resources (Ireland/Mozambique)

- **What they do**: Operates the Moma titanium minerals mine in Mozambique, one of the world's largest. Kenmare is the fourth-largest global producer of titanium feedstocks (ilmenite and rutile).Wikipedia
- **Why they stand out**: Their product—titanium dioxide pigment—is widely used in paper, paint, plastics, and other major industries.Popular Mechanics+4Wikipedia+4MINING.COM+4

4. Major Diversified Mining Giants

These industry powerhouses span a broad range of earth-based minerals:

- **Glencore** (Switzerland)
- **Jiangxi Copper** (China)
- **BHP Group** (Australia)
- **Rio Tinto** (U.K.)
- **Vale SA** (Brazil)
- **Anglo American** (U.K.)
- **Zijin Mining** (China), and othersBarron's+15Investopedia+15Exoswan Insights+15

Notable highlights:

- **Anglo American** is the world's largest platinum producer and a major diamond, copper, nickel, and iron ore producer.Wikipedia
- **Rio Tinto** is the third-largest diamond miner globally, with operations in Canada and Zimbabwe.Wikipedia

Why Earth-Based Mineral Companies Matter

1. **Strategic Technologies**: Critical minerals like rare earths and titanium are fundamental to electric vehicles, defense systems, renewable energy, semiconductors, and medical devices.
2. **Supply Chain Diversification**: With China dominating major segments—especially rare-earth processing—companies like MP Materials and Lynas are pivotal to diversifying global supply chains.Exoswan Insights+7Barron's+7Barron's+7
3. **Industrial Backbone**: Giants like BHP and Glencore support global manufacturing and infrastructure needs with metals like copper, iron, gold, and more.Investopedia
4. **Sustainability & Oversight**: Large diversified miners are increasingly under pressure to improve ESG standards and environmental performance.groupcaliber.com

Summary Table

Company / Group	Country / Region	Key Earth-Based Minerals / Focus
MP Materials	USA	Rare earths (NdPr), processing, magnet production
Lynas Rare Earths	Australia/Malaysia/USA	Rare earth mining and refining (heavy rare earths)
Kenmare Resources	Ireland/Mozambique	Titanium feedstocks (ilmenite, rutile)
Diversified Mining Giants	Global (e.g., BHP, Glencore, Rio Tinto, Anglo American)	Copper, platinum, iron ore, diamonds, etc.

Chapter 32:
FINALLY, I leave you with some poetry based on my REAL-LIFE experiences…

1) *THE BLOOD RED RAIN (FOR THOSE THAT MIGHT BE INCARCERATED)*

2) *FOUR CLOVERS WE NOT (FOR THOSE THAT LISTEN TO THE NEWS)*

3) *ON ANGEL WINGS (FOR THOSE THAT WILL NEED HELP)*

4) *RISE ABOVE (FOR THE ONES THAT MAY FAIL AND NEED TO GET BACK IN THE RACE)*

5) *WHAT TYPE OF FRIEND WOULD YOU BE? (FOR ALL OF US WHO ARE TRUSTWORTHY OF OTHERS)*

6) *AMERICA WHERE DREAMS MARCH ON (FOR ALL OF US WHO HAVE DREAMS)*

The Blood Red Rain

by Riccardo Marini -2016

Lonely dark nights, knights that wander
Cunning beasts that pace and ponder

Dripping sweat and drooling saliva
Quenching their thirst for blood, they hunger

Gladiators with make-shift swords
Cheering spectators wanting more

Ranting cuttings! Cuttings! Conquistadors
Hour by hour, a list is drawn

Who shall commit mortal sin once more?
A forgotten mother lost first born

The revolving door spits two men
To fight a battle nobody wins, nobody mourns

Barron and bright the sun burns
At the Bare Hill Prison, inmates scorn

Beyond, beyond, some seagulls fly
Landing on a rusted, tin rooftop, nearby

Peering through wired windows with a grimaced grin
A feud of crazed minds begins
A collision spawn

Danger boils and tempers flare
The anger, anger, twister spins

The crazed malaise settles in
Throughout the beige metal bins

At half past midnight
Under snow white linen

The red stain razor's pain begins
You can hear the swish of slashing
Through thick and thin

The sparks of spears,

the thud of thunder

The spikes of sinister,
Pierce one-to-other,
With torrential hatred
One day to another

The blood red rain floods within
It pours, pours, and pours

The Bare Hill River overflows
A slice of life
Some got to know
And some seagulls watched in woe.

"Four Clovers We Not"
by Riccardo Marini 2020

Our skins have whelked
Our soul's un-wealed
Our future betrayed
With broken promises once made

Our tears can't abate
The road of indifference we take
We wonder what awaits
We wonder our fates

Gone for now, the coral reefs
The dust unsettled beneath our feet
An angry earth in grief
An angry earth in grief

The veil of beauty now feigned
The fountain of youth poisoned in vain
All in our sands of time
Only a few grains remain

Spinning, spinning faster than slow
The Northern lights no longer aglow
The oceans overflow
The magnetic field reversed

The sun scorches and burns, scorches and burns
The hurricane winds of time
They blow, they blow
Till nothing stays the same
Someone is changing our game

The wars still fight for the infamous government fools
The bullets still fly, the guns still rule
But the dead that are found
Are the children in our schools

The landscape changed, we await, we await
Our words define new meaning in our times

What once meant this, now means that
We can't seem to syncopate

The sidewalk crack, now a drug
My mother's pot, now a smoke
A bottle of coke, now a snort

We give birth to new words that hurt, that hurt

Nika and Covid, Sars and Mers
Al-Qaida and cli-fi galore
Death at doorsteps DuJour
We become the next dinosaurs

Our wrinkles and scars reflect
The custody and oversight
Of another stepchild in neglect
The abuse few will forget

Overwhelmed with mind fatigue
Widgets and gadgets all we see
But not our indiscretions
Against you or me

Higgledy-piggledy
Biggety we be
Four Clovers we not
Four Clovers we not.

On Angel Wings

by Riccardo Marini, 2024

I was flying, but couldn't land
Like a bird without feet
I was flying asleep.

Too young to understand
Life has the upper hand
I, just an ordinary man
Reaching for cherché

Flying and flying above
Flying and flying above
I never stopped; I never wept

Cherché, cherché
With broken wings
And broken heart
With obscured vision
Like a blind man in the dark

Without a destination
Without a plan
Mentally fatigued

How could I ever land
After all, I had no feet
My fate a pool of quicksand

Through wind, rain, and storm
I asked, "Where did I belong?
Like a bird without feet
I was flying asleep

'Till you came along,
Till you came along

You gave me guidance
You gave me strength
As I rested on your wings,
As I rested on your wings

We soared and soared and soared
We flew above the heavens
And landed on your Angel Wings
Cherché, cherché

Rise Above

by Riccardo Marini – 2015

I spent my days sliding on the distant tenuous hills of worry
Approaching closer to a daily path of
Unsurmountable mountains I was forced to climb.

Far away from the fields of peaceful glory
I envisioned in my mind
I struggled not to slip on the rocks' ledge

Many times, I faulted and fell into
the valley of despair, eagerly waiting below.
Never had a moment of heartfelt rest
Battered, bruised, and bloodied,

I resumed my seemingly endless quest.
Every morning, I awoke
to be faced with the cold winds of life

The rains bitterly stung my face like spikes
Fear was my morning ray of light
it peered through the tempestuous clouds of doubt

It affected my very being,
Like a thief in the night,
robbing my spirit, raping my soul.

Others around enjoyed their sunny life,
I inwardly suffered in silence with every blow
I choose the path of naivety and trust

I had reached the crossroads of no return.
I had traveled terrains and destinations unknown.
Neither a compass, nor training or defense

I could not stand still, I forged ahead.
The struggles were not new
Many were set by trailblazers I foolishly followed.

Not a sip of water in my empty flask
Walking barefoot on shattered glass
Never a restful night's sleep

Often awakened by broken promises
Vanished dreams in thin air

Scarily wondering how I would fare
BUT LIKE AN UNKNOWN MYSTICAL FORCE
I surrendered myself to assist some other I placed before me.

Cashing in would wait for a later date.
Foolishly watched my assets slip from my grip.
Mis-calculated the time I had,

Cost of compound interest for bad decisions once made.
Silent hidden enemies lay in wait
An ambush at dark was my fate

My resolve to weather the storms of time
The droughts of failure, the famine of success
Poor emotionally vested acquaintances once called family and friends

All with time heals the wounds
The scars may still be seen
 I, and fel my heart
A remembrance of the past

The peaceful fields of glory envisioned now I stand
I see the sunrise I eagerly love and befriend.
I Rise Above. I Rise Above.

What Kind of Friend Would You Be?
by Riccardo Marini - 2024

If you were my dream friend
What would I find at the end?

Would I find you on a dusty, boring, unswept corner room
Or, perhaps on my mind's forgotten shelf of forgotten gloom?

Would I find you in bright lights, performing to a crowd
Without me standing alongside the stage?

Would you be endowed?
With an imagination that creates fireworks when you speak.

Or would you have fallen
Into a molded basement suitcase lying around all by yourself?

Would you carry secrets to my grave?
Or would you share them to my face?

Would your message be distracting from emotion?
Sadly, void of grace?
Or would it be cheerfully nice? Which I could share

Would you fabricate, creating a thrill for my pleasure?
Or would you not care how I felt to any measure?

Would you be my soul's confidant?
Or, happy to observe from a distance
My anxiety, my struggles that you might mitigate

Would you examine the frightful thoughts I've buried deeply
In the valleys of my mind?
And build me a staircase to help bring them to the surface
To deal with my sublime?

Would your insightful poetic writings make me feel like a bird in flight?
Or would your character display deceit,
Would you hide yourself if I came calling for an important task

In need in the middle of the night
Would you lie under our oath?
Would you steal the gold from my teeth?

Would you watch me kneel in grief
Crying a river of tears beneath my feet

Or would you build a dam to hold back the flood
So, someday you will open the gates
With pleasure and watch me drown

Or would you enter my soul
With a bucket and mop
and take as long as it would take
To dry it all up?

And if you could gift yourself to anyone in the world,
Who would you choose?
Me or someone else?

Could you bleed every last drop
To give to me?
And no one else?

Could you read me a love story
Holding my hand as I fell asleep

Cause I would like to know
What kind of friend would you be?

"America, Where Dreams March On" by Riccardo Marini – July 2025

Cascading fire waterfalls
Of red, white, and blue
With golden opportunities for one and all

Blazing twilight skies in flame
Each star a tribute to our freedom's name
Our Glory, our story is bold and true
America, where dreams come marching through

Overflowing rivers surge about
Carrying the hopes of millions
Whose dreams echo throughout

Bravery flows like raging tides
As every loss our pride abides

Soldiers' shoulders squared and tight
Eyes lifted high above their battle scars.
Standing on mountains of courage every night

Their voices carried by the winds of time
They swim in oceans of braveness in heart
Without hesitate, they fight with mighty faith

Waves shaped by service, resilience and grace
They are all in; their roots run deep when they begin
Their price is blood, limb, and skin

They cross prairies wide with sacrifice
With the footsteps of perseverance
Across planted seeds of destiny galore
Once planted by ancestors before

My America shines so bright
With vision, bold and right
In every grain sowed
Our citizens bestowed

Green valleys' stretch beyond the horizon of promise
Brimming with the pulse of great innovations

Where a thought becomes an invention
And effort gives rise to change and spirit

Bridges span deep divides
Built with the wisdom of age,
Steel, stone, and pride

And the curiosity of youth
Gaping generations now friends
Gather as one in our promise land

Our streets are not paved with gold,
But, cemented with beacons of light
Torches of success carried by young souls
Lighting our tomorrows with fearless intent

Endless shores shimmer in the sun
Each grain of sand, a dream imagined
A hope whispered, a promise made
A heart inspired

We're not flawless
But ever striving
Woven from our strength

Men, Women and Children
Stitched together with belief
Of God's faith they befriend

That no goal is too wild
No voice too small to rise
And no dream is unrealized

     In America

     Where Dreams March On

     Where Dreams March On

"Our Torch Charlie Kirk"

By Riccardo Marini – September 2025

He stood for God, for family, for love,
A messenger of light, sent from above.
Through campus halls and crowded squares,
He spoke with courage, his heart laid bare.

A modern Jesus, spreading his word
With dignity, grace, and faith at his side,
He carried the truth with nothing to hide.

The morning sun rose bright and clear,
A father, a husband, a son we held dear.
He carried our torch with nothing to fear

The young cheered, his message of hope,
A nation inspired, a reason to cope.
Yet far on a rooftop, hidden from sight,
Crawled evil's shadow, prepared to strike.

Without a warning, the rifle's breath,
Delivered its venom, a sentence of death.
His blood red on white fences near,
Staining the soil we hold so dear.

Silence tried to steal the sounds
A battle cry so sincere all around
A bright beacon now downed

The mirrors of faith shattered in pain,
As dreams for tomorrow, we struggled to sustain.
The pain of rain, like storms of tears from the sky,
Hearts pierced with sorrow, yet refusing to die.

His words shall echo through the valleys of time,
Carved in our memory's mountain peaks,
Etched into rhyme.

We walk hand in hand
We'll carry your message with a thunderous drum,
Until every serpent retreats under the rock it's from.

For though one man falls, his devotion shall never depart
His Love shall never lay, His truth shall not cease
His dream shall never die, His light shall never fade
His spirit lives on in our courage and our continued peace every day.
Our Torch Charlie Kirk

MY RECOMMENDED READINGS....

RICCARDO MARINI - "A POET'S PALLETE OF HIS SOUL"

ALEX GAMBINO

"100 NOTORIOUS ORGANIZED CRIME FIGURES AROUND THE WORLD"

ZIG ZIGLAR - "SEE YOU AT THE TOP"

THOMAS J WOLF - "THE MAN IN THE GLASS"

DR LAYNE LONGFELLOW - "THE STRESS OF SUCCESS"

Bill O'Rielly Books

Confronting Evil
Confronting the Presidents
Killing Regan
Killing the Mob
Killing England
Killing the Rising Sun
Killing the Killers
Killing the Witches
Killing the Legends
Killing Lincoln
Killing the SS
Killing Crazy Horse
The Day the President Was Shot
The United States of Trump

www.ingramcontent.com/pod-product-compliance
Lightning Source LLC
Chambersburg PA
CBHW052341210326
41597CB00037B/6217